The Library of American Biography

EDITED BY OSCAR HANDLIN

Daniel Webster
and the
Rise of
National Conservatism

Richard N. Current

Daniel Webster
and the
Rise of
National Conservatism

Edited by Oscar Handlin

Little, Brown and Company · *Boston* · *Toronto*

LIBRARY OF CONGRESS CATALOG CARD NO. 54–7468

F

Published simultaneously in Canada
by Little, Brown & Company (Canada) Limited

PRINTED IN THE UNITED STATES OF AMERICA

To
Rose

Editor's Preface

AFTER 1810 new personalities and new issues came to dominate the American political scene. A new generation moved to the forefront of events, and in the next half century confronted the consequences of tremendous territorial and economic changes. As the nation's boundaries reached westward to the Pacific and as the plantation and factory system recast the modes of production, the problems of politics took on a fresh configuration.

Often the troubled men of these decades were tempted to look back upon their predecessors with envy. The issues, it seemed, had been much clearer in the Revolutionary years when the common British enemy had drawn the nation together, when it was possible to define tyranny and liberty in simple terms, and when the pressure of crisis had given a plain meaning to the common interest of the commonwealth. In the retrospective view of the later era, the actual divisions of the earlier period faded away and left an impressive appearance of harmony and unity.

A sad contrast indeed with their own days! The War of 1812, unlike that of 1776, came to an inglorious end; and thereafter conflicting interests wrangled interminably

about the tariff or the currency, about internal improvements and the bank, while the portentous slavery issue
reaching into the territories seemed to threaten the future
of the Union itself. Often enough the question was asked
whether the descendants of the Revolutionary patriots
were fulfilling the promises of their valiant ancestors.

In some sections of the country the heady currents of
expansion were exciting enough to still occasional qualms
on this account. But the merchants and the prosperous
country squires of New England felt a growing unease at
the course of national development. Having earned their
wealth in the flush post-Revolutionary decades, they
sought stability, whether in trade or in the newly developing industries. As the country grew and their section lost
in relative importance, they came to fear the impetuous actions of wild new men heedless of established personal and
property rights. Yet even the most perturbed of the New
Englanders found it difficult to surrender the democratic
faith that was their heritage from the Revolution. Rather
they longed for some saving line of action and body of
ideas that would temper the will of the majority with respect for property rights and the interests of minorities —
including their own. Their point of departure was the political theory of John Adams and his Revolutionary contemporaries; under the pressure of the practical necessities
of their own time the New England merchants contrived
from it a conception of national conservatism that has had
continuing significance to our own times.

Daniel Webster played a crucial role in this development. Himself the product of the New England back
country and the son of a family of Federalist squires, he
entered in early life upon an intimate association with the

merchants of Boston for whom he was often to speak in national affairs. Thereafter his career was inextricably bound up with the most important events of the period that led to the Civil War.

His colorful life is instructive, however, for more than the light it throws on that fateful period. His experience reveals also the difficulties and dilemmas encountered by the men in our past who wished to work out a conservative philosophy for American politics. From that point of view Richard Current's incisive analysis has a direct and continuing pertinence for the citizens of a democratic republic.

OSCAR HANDLIN

Contents

Contents

Daniel Webster
and the
Rise of
National Conservatism

I
Substance, Not Form
1782-1816

"We are, sir, from principle and habit, attached to the Union of the states. But our attachment is to the substance, and not to the form."

IN THE BEGINNING both nature and man were kind to Daniel Webster. Though frail and sickly as a boy, with a head a bit large for his body, he had the makings of one of America's most magnificent physical specimens; and that oversized head contained a brain with startling powers of assimilation and retention. His childhood was happy, and throughout his life he clung with more than ordinary fondness to his early memories. He was born on January 18, 1782. The world he first knew, in the valley of the Merrimack, near the middle of New Hampshire, to others seemed inhospitable with its long, deep winters and its granite hills. But he remembered best its inviting aspects — the summer sun and shade in the woods and on the waters about his father's farm, which lay on meadowland along the riverbank. It was, for him, a world of welldisposed people. He seldom lacked attention and appreciation as he grew up.

He did not want for inspiration, either. His father was a man to stir the pride of any son. Ebenezer Webster, six feet six, with his broad shoulders and full chest, his Roman nose, his black hair and eyes and his skin almost as dark, looked the born soldier and frontiersman that he was. After fighting with Rogers's Rangers in the French and Indian War, he pioneered on the upper Merrimack, then went off to command a company in the Revolution. Back home again in Salisbury, Captain Webster farmed and kept a tavern while filling one role after another in the public life of the town: highway surveyor, moderator of the town meeting, selectman, town clerk, coroner, judge. As a delegate to the state convention of 1788, he voted to ratify the new Federal Constitution, and as a presidential elector the next year he cast his ballot for his old acquaintance of Revolutionary days, George Washington.

From his father, Daniel heard many a story of the early settlers, of red men and redcoats, of far-off things and battles long ago. Daniel became a man of peace, not war, yet all his life he delighted in that lore of fighting, revered the sites of historic bloodshed, and treasured such relics as the two silver buttons his father had picked up on the battlefield of Bennington. He felt honored when old General Stark told him he had, like Captain Webster, a complexion most suitable for a soldier, one so dark that burned gunpowder would not change it.

From his father he also heard about the great men of the country, and much indeed about the greatest of them all, who was first in war, first in peace, and first in Daniel's heart. When President Washington lost the support of Thomas Jefferson, and politics divided people into Federalists and Republicans, there could be no more question about Daniel's sympathies than about his father's. "Carry me back home!" the aging captain was supposed to have cried when he fell sick in a village that had gone for Jefferson. "I don't want to die in a Republican town."

Among Ebenezer Webster's ten children, five of whom were born to his first wife and five to his second, Daniel was the youngest except for one girl. He loved the farm but not the labor of it, and his brothers and sisters, like his father, yielded to his winning ways which, as much as his physical weakness, often enabled him to escape the more irksome family chores. His favorite brother, Ezekiel, did his own work and much of Daniel's too. Once, at haying time, when Daniel could not or would not "hang" (adjust) his scythe to satisfy his father, the latter told him to hang it to suit himself, so he hung it in a tree and went off to play with one of his sisters, while everybody laughed.

He liked nothing better than an appreciative audience, and as an expert reader, he was always ready to perform. His mother or his older sisters had taught him his letters from the Bible when he was very young, or so he afterward supposed, though he could not recollect how or when he had learned to read. To teamsters stopping at his father's tavern he recited from the Scriptures while he watered their horses, and these men were much taken with the bright lad they knew as "little Black Dan." An illiterate Yorkshireman, a deserter from the British army, who lived with his wife on a corner of the Webster farm, depended on Daniel to read him newspaper accounts of England's fortunes in the war with France. Years later Webster apostrophized his long-gone Yorkshire friend: "Thou hast carried me many a mile on thy back, paddled me over, and over, and up and down the stream, and given whole days in aid of my boyish sports, and asked no meed, but that, at night, I would sit down at thy cottage door, and read to thee some passage of thy country's glory!"

Daniel received the best of his early education from newspapers that the occasional post rider brought, from the political gossip of wayfarers at the farmhouse tavern, from his mother's Bible, and from the books in the circulating library his father had helped to found. When well enough he also went to school at the different houses, sometimes two or three miles away, where the schoolmaster boarded in succession around the township. He won prizes for his excellence at the rote-learning of that day, quickly memorizing long strings of Biblical verses or stanzas from the hymnal.

At thirteen, as a casual helper in the local lawyer's office, he picked up a Latin grammar, committed it to memory, and made such an impression that his employer insisted he should go on to an academy. To Exeter the captain accordingly took his son, shod in clumsy cowhide and dressed in homespun which no longer fitted. Here, away from home, Daniel for the first time failed to shine. Dreading the ridicule of his more sophisticated classmates, the orator-to-be was too weak and nervous even to get up and open his mouth when his turn at declamation came. After a couple of terms, the family funds ran low and he quit Exeter; at fifteen he was teaching a country school not far from home. Again a *deus ex machina* intervened, this time in the person of a neighboring minister of the gospel, who declared that Daniel's talents marked him for college and who offered to prepare him for it.

Though Webster's phrase later described it as a "small

college," Dartmouth was actually a large and flourishing institution, numbering nearly a hundred and fifty students and graduating larger classes than any of its contemporaries except Harvard. Among his fellow students in Hanover the youth from Salisbury, now growing into robust and handsome manhood, soon found a satisfying place. He did well enough in the classroom, though he was too casual with his studies to become a top scholar. He stood out above all the rest in the most highly esteemed competitive sport, which was public speaking.

His reputation reached the local villagers, and while yet a junior he was invited to deliver their Fourth of July address. "I had not then learned," he apologized in after years, "that all true power in writing is in the idea, not in the style." And the style at Hanover, on that July 4, 1800, was perhaps a little overdone (though less bombastic than in hundreds of other places on the same day). But the ideas, if unoriginal, were good enough to appeal to the strong Federalist proclivities of the campus and the community in 1800, and good enough for Webster to repeat with variations for half a century thereafter: the beauties of the Federal Constitution; the "virtuous manner" in which it had been administered by President Washington and his successor John Adams; the blessings of peace in the United States, while war continually devastated Europe; the expansion of the "gentle empire" of science and learning from Maine to Florida; the special destiny of America, "designed to be inhabited by a nobler race of men."

After his graduation Webster spent several years in rather desultory preparation for a legal career. He read law with the attorney at home, then taught school in Fryeburg, Maine, and finally took the bold step of going all the way to Boston and introducing himself to one of the city's most distinguished advocates, Christopher Gore. He won his way immediately into the good graces of the ge-nial Gore, who became his instructor, patron, and friend. An ardent anti-Jeffersonian, long resident in England, Gore confirmed him in his preference for the Federalist party as against the Republican and for English ways as opposed to French.

A gentleman of well-cultivated tastes, Gore also intro-duced him to some of the delights of good living. Once, when Webster was unwell, Gore asked him how he lived, and Webster said he fared rather poorly at his humble lodgings, ate corned beef and cabbage, drank nothing ex-cept plain water. "That will not do," said Gore. "You must drink a glass of good wine occasionally." Webster replied: "I cannot afford to drink wine." Taking the hint, Gore began to supply him with occasional bottles from a well-stocked garret. "I recovered my health," Webster re-lated more than forty years afterward. "But, alas! like a be-leaguered city which is compelled to call in the aid of auxiliary forces, I repulsed the enemy; but, the auxiliaries having established themselves in the citadel, I have never been able to dispossess them."

Gore helped his protégé to make a decision that was crucial to the latter's career. Daniel's father needed finan-cial support in his old age, the college education of his sons — Ezekiel as well as Daniel — having left a burden of debt. By teaching school Daniel had helped with Eze-kiel's college expenses and had contributed something, but not enough, toward paying off the mortgage. Both the Webster boys spent faster than they could earn or beg or borrow. "Money, Daniel, money," Ezekiel once appealed from Dartmouth, adding: "It is a fact, Dan, that I was called on for a dollar, where I owed it, and borrowed it, and have borrowed it four times since, to pay those I borrowed it of." At last, while Daniel was in Boston, his father got him the clerkship of the county court at home, a job worth fifteen hundred a year in fees. But Gore persuaded him to finish his studies instead of accepting it. Daniel took the edge off his father's disappointment by borrowing several hundred dollars in Boston to meet the most pressing of the family bills.

After completing his studies he opened what he cynically called a shop "for the manufacture of justice writs" in Boscawen, which was near enough home for him to be able to look out for his parents and the farm. "My business," he wrote, "has been just about so-so; its quantity less objectionable than its quality." Much of it consisted of collecting debts for certain creditors (other than his own), including merchants in distant Boston. After two years of this, his father having died meanwhile, he moved in 1807 to New Hampshire's seaport and metropolis — Portsmouth — which with its population of five thousand was then the twelfth largest city in the United States and a likely place for an ambitious young lawyer.

But not an easy place! Webster had to make his way among a number of extremely able and well-established practitioners at the Portsmouth bar. Greatest of them, and one of the greatest in the whole country, was Jeremiah Mason, a giant in intellect as well as physique and a shrewd pleader who conversed with jurymen in their own language. He became a personal friend, though a professional rival, and taught Webster something of the art of plain talk. But he found in Webster certain abilities that he himself could not match, observing once in admiration that a remarkable actor was lost to the stage when Daniel Webster took up law. A less friendly New Hampshire lawyer, William Plumer, wrote of Webster, when the latter had been in Portsmouth only three years and was still in his twenties: "As a speaker merely he is perhaps the best at the bar. His language is correct, his gestures good, and his delivery slow, articulate, and distinct. He excels in the statement of facts; but he is not thought to be a deep read lawyer. His manners are not pleasing — being haughty, cold, and overbearing."

In the spring of 1808 Webster had revisited the Merrimack Valley and brought back a bride. Grace Fletcher, a preacher's daughter and a part-time schoolmistress, was a year older than he. Her affectionate and thoughtful ways made her attractive despite the plainness of her features. Rather shy, Mrs. Webster set off the brilliance of her husband in the drawing rooms of their fashionable friends, where his manners, rapidly acquiring polish, were more pleasing than in the courts of law. Unfortunately for her, he was away a good deal of the time while he traveled the circuit in New Hampshire. And his absences lengthened when he went into politics.

By the time his political career began, his preferences and principles were, in their essentials, already fixed. The world, as he had known it, was on the whole good. He saw no reason to reject the ideals of his father. Not that he resisted "progress" — far from it — but he was inclined to think that things ought to be kept pretty much as they were, except where there was some direct material gain to be had by changing them. He thought of himself as a conservative.

2

The merchants and shipowners of Portsmouth, with whose interests Webster at once identified his own, were prospering in 1807 as never before — and never again. They were making money out of the Napoleonic Wars, out of the necessities of Great Britain and France, both of which depended on the Yankees for much of their carrying trade. But the business had become risky. Caught between Napoleon's decrees and Parliament's orders in council, American vessels clearing for the European continent took the chance of capture by the British, and those bound to or from a British port risked seizure by the French. Hundreds were caught and confiscated, the majority by the British, who also stopped American ships to take off crewmen, naturalized and even native-born, as alleged deserters from the Royal Navy.

To decrease their risks and losses, American shipowners desired a bigger and more active Navy for the United States. "If we will have commerce, we must protect it," spoke up Webster as their coming advocate. "There is a system which is opposed to every degree of naval preparation. There are men who would not defend commerce an inch beyond the land." This system, so "impracticable and absurd," was the Jeffersonian one, that of the Republicans, so devoted to the agricultural interest that they disregarded the commercial.

President Jefferson did not go far enough, and yet he went too far, to suit the men of commerce. On the issue of impressment he refused to compromise with England. This issue roused the martial spirit of most Americans throughout the country when His Majesty's ship *Leopard* fired on the U.S.S. *Chesapeake* — not a merchantman but a man-of-war — and took off several members of the crew. To bring the British and at the same time the French to terms, without war, Jefferson (at the instance of his Secretary of State, James Madison) decided to exert economic pressure on both belligerents by keeping American ships at home. Congress passed his embargo bill and added a "force act" to see that the prohibition was obeyed.

The embargo brought depression to the lately bustling waterfronts at Portsmouth and elsewhere along the northeastern coast. Shipowners and merchants, forgetting their vexation at the British and the French, turned to hating Thomas Jefferson. Again stating their case for them, Webster put forth an anonymous pamphlet in which he denied the constitutionality of the embargo. "The Government of the United States is a delegated, *limited* Government," he wrote. The Constitution had given Congress the power only to regulate commerce, not to destroy it as in the recent law. "This, it would seem, is not regulating commerce by an Embargo. It is, in effect, carrying on war, at the expense of one class of the community."

Just before Jefferson left the presidency his unpopular embargo was repealed, but his *alter ego* and successor, President Madison, tried other experiments in economic warfare and eventually war itself. The war cry of free seas and sailors' rights arose not from northeastern seaports but from the frontier settlements of the South and West. Many frontiersmen looked to hostilities with England as an occasion for conquering territory — Canada, Florida — so as to remove the border Indian menace and also, perhaps, to get new farming land. In the fall of 1811 they

fired the first shot, in a battle with the Indians at Tippecanoe, and the War Hawks in Congress renewed their
clamor for war with the power presumably behind the
hostile Indians. Yielding to this pressure within his party,
President Madison became increasingly more sensitive to
British than to French infringements of maritime rights.
When Napoleon pretended to exempt Americans from his
decrees, Madison imposed an embargo against Great Britain alone. When the British still delayed the repeal of
their orders in council, and still refused to renounce their
impressment claims, he asked Congress for a war declaration, which came on June 18, 1812.

On July 4, Webster spoke before the Portsmouth chapter of the Washington Benevolent Society, an organization
of New England Federalists who agitated against the party
in power as disloyal to the Washingtonian past. "The
voice of the whole mercantile interest is united, to an unprecedented degree, against the war, which is declared to
be undertaken, at so much hazard of blood and treasure,
for their benefit," Webster told the society. "Resistance
and insurrection form no part of our creed," he went on
to explain. "If we are taxed, to carry on this war, we shall
pay. If our personal services are required, we shall yield
them to the precise extent of our constitutional liability.
By the exercise of our constitutional right of suffrage, by
the peaceable remedy of election, we shall seek to restore
wisdom to our councils, and peace to our country."

In August, when the Federalists of Rockingham County
met in convention, Webster presented and they endorsed
a public letter addressed to James Madison, Esquire,
President of the United States. Ominously this Rockingham Memorial announced: "We shrink from the separa-

tion of the states, as an event fraught with incalculable
evils, and it is among our strongest objections to the present course of measures, that they have, in our opinion, a
very dangerous and alarming bearing on such an event."
That is to say, if a separation should occur the administration and its adherents South and West would be to blame.
The event could happen only when "one portion of the
country" undertook "to control, to regulate, and to sacrifice the interest of another," only when a "small and heated
majority" disregarded the rights of a "large and respectable minority," as the Republicans had done. On this platform Webster was nominated for Congress. He was easily
elected.

3

In Washington on a May day in 1813 the neophyte congressman from New Hampshire went to the White House
to make his bow to the President. "I did not like his
looks," Webster wrote back home, "any better than I like
his Administration." He wrote in a jocular tone, and yet
he meant what he said. During the next two years he did
his best to destroy the administration and all its works
and, in particular, to sabotage what Federalists called
"Mr. Madison's War."

The war went none too well. Repeated efforts to drive
the British out of Canada failed ignominiously. At first
Americans won a series of spectacular victories in naval
duels on the high seas, but in time the Royal Navy reas-
serted its supremacy, set up a tight blockade of the Atlan-

tic coast, and landed invading troops at several points. The United States was on the defensive.

The Republicans in Washington labored to salvage what they could from their hapless venture, both by military and by diplomatic efforts. Early in the war the outstanding War Hawk, Henry Clay of Kentucky, embarked for Ghent as a member of a commission delegated to negotiate peace. In the House of Representatives the leadership of the administration forces fell to another jingo, the intense young John C. Calhoun from South Carolina, who devoted himself to justifying the war and raising men and money with which to fight it. At every step he ran against the Federalist obstructionists, foremost among them Webster. The two brilliant champions of their respective sections fought a series of verbal contests, the first of many that were to engage the attention of a whole generation of the American people, Calhoun speaking with the staccato effect of a rapid-fire gun, Webster more slowly and sonorously, his words vibrant with emotion.

The gentleman from New Hampshire, introducing resolution after resolution to embarrass the administration, demanded reasons for the war and intimated that Napoleon had tricked the President into antagonizing England, as in fact Napoleon had. Every measure to finance the fighting — by loans, taxes, tariffs, or a national bank — Webster and his Federalist allies vehemently denounced. At a time when volunteering lagged and the Army was seriously undermanned, he opposed a bill to encourage enlistments, but he professed to disagree not so much with the war itself as with the way it was being fought. "If, then, the war must be continued," he declaimed, "go to the ocean. If you are seriously contending for maritime rights, go to the theatre where alone those rights can be defended."

He seemed to view defeat on the battlefield as a misfortune of the party in power, not of the country, and certainly not of the Federalists or himself. He wrote privately (in the summer of 1813): "The fact is, the Administration are, for the moment, confounded. They are hard pushed in our house — much harder in the Senate. They are in a sad pickle. Who cares?" Even when the worst occurred, when (in the summer of 1814) invading troops drove the government out of Washington and burned the public buildings, he changed his tone a bit but not his tack.

The winter of 1814-1815 brought the republic apparently to the verge of ruin. "If Peace does not come this winter," Daniel told his brother Ezekiel, "the Govt. will die in its own weakness." In Hartford a group of New England Federalists met to demand constitutional reforms, seemingly as the price of their section's remaining in the Union. Webster himself had nothing to do with the Hartford Convention, except to advise the governor of New Hampshire against sending delegates, and the state was not officially represented, though two of its counties were. But he kept up his obstructionist activities in the House at Washington, while the government grew increasingly desperate.

In its extremity the administration decided to draft men into the regular army from the militia, which in some of the New England states the governors ordered not to fight. The conscription bill was lost when Webster rose in the House (December 9, 1814) to launch his rumbling oratory. The draft, he argued, was unconstitutional. True, Congress had power to raise armies but not by any means, however violent, that it might choose. Congress also had the power to borrow money but not, thereby, the right to impose a forced loan. Though not limited by specific clauses of the Constitution, these powers were restrained by the general spirit of the whole document, and a "free constitution" must be construed only according to "free principles." The draft — "this horrible lottery" — was worse than unconstitutional. It was criminal: ". . . 'tis murder."

No such law could ever be carried out, Webster warned. "The operation of measures thus unconstitutional and illegal ought to be prevented by a resort to other measures which are both constitutional and legal. It will be the solemn duty of the state governments to protect their own authority over their own militia and to interpose between their citizens and arbitrary power." This kind of interposition between the Federal government and their own people was one of the "highest obligations" of the states, Webster averred, and then to prove his point he quoted from the New Hampshire bill of rights. His people would fight — but only for their freedom. "If administration has found that it can not form an army without conscription, it will find, if it venture on these experiments, that it can not enforce conscription without an army."

Webster referred to "the state of things in New England," meaning in particular the assembling of the Federalists at Hartford, and denied that they were in any sense disunionists. "Those who cry out that the Union is in danger," he maintained, "are themselves the authors of that danger. They put its existence to hazard by measures of violence, which it is not capable of enduring." That was to say, the Republicans of the South and West themselves had brought the country to its dire pass, against the counsels of true unionists. "They alone, Sir, are friends to the union of the states who endeavor to maintain the principles of civil liberty in the country, and to preserve the spirit in which the Union was framed."

After this speech Webster grimly rejoiced in private that the government could not collect taxes, borrow money, or recruit soldiers. "What can it do?" he asked. "The Govt. *cannot last,* under this war & in the hands of these men, another twelve month. Not that the opposition will break it down, but it will break itself down. It will go out."

He soon was disappointed. Just two days after he had written down his "sober opinion," Henry Clay and the other peacemakers in Ghent signed a treaty which, when ratified, would end the war. News of the signing, on the day before Christmas, did not reach Washington until after the dispatches telling of Andrew Jackson's smashing victory, January 8, 1815, over the invading British at New Orleans. These tidings of victory and peace embarrassed and refuted the delegation arriving from Hartford with the Federalist hint that the Republicans must reform or perish, along perhaps with the Union itself. The American people got the impression that their country had won the war, and in their eyes the Federalist party was discredited as almost treasonable.

4

In fact the Federalist threat had been rather empty, only a few Hartford dissidents actually favoring secession, even as a last resort. The party could not act as a unit, in New England or elsewhere, for diverging economic interests set its members against one another. Embargo, nonintercourse laws, and war, though costing merchants and shipowners much of their market and their carrying trade, stimulated the growth of banking and manufacturing and the transfer of capital to these newer enterprises. Men with money still in shipping came to realize that their profits depended largely on the national market, the coastal trade. Only a minority held to the narrowly sectional views that most had entertained during the war.

Re-elected to Congress, Webster represented a constituency still unready to accept all the nationalizing tendencies coming into focus in postwar Washington. In the main he disapproved the program of the Republicans, led by Calhoun and Clay, who advocated a kind of national planning for both prosperity and defense. According to their scheme, the government was to expand the home market and increase the military strength of the country by building roads and waterways, re-establishing a national bank (the original one having expired in 1811), and putting up a high protective tariff. Federalists could see a partisan advantage in supporting Federal aid to internal improvements, since Republicans disagreed among themselves on that issue, and Webster voted for Calhoun's improvements bill, which Madison vetoed.

In regard to the bank, the question was what kind to
set up. The administration desired an institution which
could lend freely to the government and could issue notes
to circulate as paper money, not redeemable in cash. But
Webster demanded a conservative, independent, specie-
paying bank. It must be one, he said, that would "command the solid capital of the country," that would attract
"men of wealth and standing" to "embark their funds" in
it. There were at that time more such men, more available funds, and more sound banks in New England than in
other sections. When the bill had been altered to suit
him, Webster voted for it.

On the tariff question he had expressed himself eloquently during the war. The duties, then doubled, were
intended to raise revenue, and the wartime acts restrict-
ing overseas trade were meant to stop Americans from
selling to the enemy. But both the tariff and the nonintercourse laws protected and encouraged such new industries
as the spinning mills of Massachusetts and Rhode Island
When Webster, in the interests of shipowners, secured the
repeal of the prohibitions on commerce, Calhoun prom-
ised the manufacturers that they would be compensated
with a general tariff law designed for outright protection.

Webster dissented. He explained (April 6, 1814) that he
was neither the enemy nor the friend of manufactures,
but he did not approve "rearing them, or any other interest, in hot-beds." He was "not in haste to see Sheffields
and Birminghams in America." Such populous manufacturing cities developed a kind of life that threatened good
morals and free governments. The factory division of labor caused workers to lose their independence to their employer. "One of these laborers, utterly incapable of making and carrying to the market on his own account the

smallest entire article, is necessarily at the mercy of the capitalist for the support of himself and family." In times of unemployment he would become a burden on society.

The old ways were better, for society and for the worker himself. "I am not anxious," Webster said, "to accelerate the approach of the period when the great mass of American labor shall not find its employment in the field; when the young men of the country shall be obliged to shut their eyes upon external nature, upon the heavens and the earth, and immerse themselves in unwholesome workshops; when they shall be obliged to shut their ears to the bleatings of their own flocks, upon their own hills, and to the voice of the lark that cheers them at the plough, that they may open them in dust, and smoke, and steam, to the perpetual whirl of spools and spindles, and the grating of rasps and saws." The true policy of government was "to suffer the different pursuits of society to take their own course, and not to give excessive bounties or encouragements to one over another." This also was the true spirit of the Constitution.

The postwar tariff controversy centered on the question of cotton goods. Shipowners of Portsmouth and of Massachusetts seaports, who imported cheap cottons from India, wished to continue their profitable trade without governmental interference, but cotton manufacturers in New England and cotton planters in the South objected to the ruinous competition of the India imports. Protectionists differed among themselves about the height and extent of the duties they required. The Boston Manufacturing Company, which operated at Waltham the first and as yet the only complete factory for both spinning and weaving in the United States, could get along with less extreme protection than its smaller competitors.

The founder of the Boston Manufacturing Company, Francis C. Lowell, member of an old merchant family and inventor of the power loom, introduced Webster to a philosophy of moderate and selective protectionism. Lowell spent the winter of 1815-1816 in Washington. "I was much with him," Webster afterwards recalled. "I found him full of exact, practical knowledge, on many subjects." The knowledgeable manufacturer remained on hand to advise the congressman during the debates on the tariff of 1816.

Webster first tried to amend the administration bill by providing for a gradual one-third reduction of the proposed new duties on cotton cloth. This, he said, would satisfy the manufacturers. But a Massachusetts member retorted that Webster spoke for a big capitalist who could stand the lower rates, which the smaller and less well established mills could not. Then Webster supported — as an act of justice to shipowners, he said — the amendment of his Federalist colleague Timothy Pickering from Salem, home port of many Indiamen, who moved to strike out the new schedule entirely and substitute the low duties of the existing law. The most that Webster could do for the India traders, however, was to get them a few months' reprieve with a provision exempting from the new tariff the cargoes of voyages already under way. He and most of the New Englanders voted against the final bill, but Calhoun and most of the South Carolinians voted for it, and it passed.

During his first decade in politics, 1807-1816, Webster had acted as if his vision seldom extended beyond the boundaries of his native New Hampshire. He made his debut in public life as a strict constructionist and an anti-nationalist. He insisted that Congress, under the Constitution, could exercise only "delegated, *limited*" powers. Advocating state rights, he carried his argument to the point of recommending a kind of nullification when he maintained that his state had a "solemn duty" to "interpose" between its citizens and the Federal government. He even hinted at secession as a justifiable recourse when a majority in the nation oppressed or tyrannized a minority within the state. And he voiced the theories of *laissez faire*, criticizing tariff protection as probably unconstitutional and certainly inexpedient.

These things he did as the agent of a fairly compact and homogeneous mercantile community. The interests he represented were to change, and so were some of his ideas. He was to spend the better part of his long career in defending principles he had attacked and condemning others he had approved during his apprentice years. But his basic conservatism was to remain with him always.

I I
Power and Property
1816-1827

"It seems to me to be plain that, in the absence of military force, political power naturally and necessarily goes into the hands which hold the property."

PORTSMOUTH, which once had aspired to outdo Boston, never recovered from the effects of the embargo and the war. As its commerce dwindled, so did the prospects of Daniel Webster. The most he could make from his law practice there was about two thousand dollars a year — not a bad salary for the time, yet not good enough for a man of his expensive habits and accumulating debts. These were increased when his house, uninsured, was destroyed by fire. Finally, in 1816, he moved with his wife and two children to Boston, the growing New England metropolis.

Boston attracted many of the most enterprising Yankees from the country towns. From New Ipswich, New Hampshire, had come the rising merchant prince Nathan Appleton, and from Groton, Massachusetts, the brothers Amos and Abbott Lawrence, founders of a leading commercial firm. Beginning as importers, Appleton and the Law-rences turned to handling domestic goods also and even-tually went into the cotton manufacturing business with Francis C. Lowell. Succeeding with their experiment at Waltham, these enterprisers bought up water rights on the lower Merrimack, started the factory town of Lowell in 1821, and vastly expanded their operations during the next several years. They set up new mills one after an-other, and new corporations to run them: the Merrimack Manufacturing Company, the Hamilton Manufacturing Company, the Appleton and Lowell companies, and still others later on.

Some of the merchants and shipowners of older Boston families, such as John Murray Forbes and Thomas Han-dasyd Perkins, also invested in the textile industry, though they continued to carry on their more glamorous but less profitable ventures overseas, to places like Smyrna and Canton. Other men of the established mercantile houses, such as Harrison Gray Otis, resisted the pecuniary attractions of the spindle and loom, and held stubbornly to the romance and respectability of the sail. So the busi-ness community of Boston remained divided for a time, but its members came increasingly to combine in common interests. Putting their profits together to erect banks as well as mills, these merchant-financiers concentrated the control of more and more New England credit into their offices on State Street.

These men the newcomer from Portsmouth represented in the law courts and, from 1823 to 1827, in Congress. They allowed him to buy stock and join the shareholders in their rather exclusive corporations. And they, along with big clients elsewhere in the country, paid him fat fees for his legal services. Soon after his arrival in Boston he was earning twenty thousand dollars a year — in a time of business depression, when common laborers made about fifty cents a day if they were lucky enough to find work at all. Yet, when he went to Congress, he borrowed about ten thousand from friends, even though he found many money-making opportunities in Washington. His fifteen-hundred-dollar salary as a congressman was insignificant, but he could take time to argue lucrative cases before the Supreme Court. And he could solicit the business of shipowners or insurance firms having claims against the government, which had assumed responsibility for some of Spain's depredations on American shipping during the French Revolutionary wars. From these "Spanish claims" he made or at least expected to make sixty thousand in a few years. During the 1820's he was probably the most highly paid lawyer in the United States.

He was also becoming the most successful orator. With the magic of the spoken word he moved judges and juries, state constitution makers, visitors and colleagues in Congress, and vast audiences gathered for special occasions. Such a brilliant performance was the first of his great occasional addresses, the Plymouth oration of 1820, commemorating the two-hundredth anniversary of the landing of the Pilgrims, that it seemed to many of his hearers almost to outshine the event it celebrated. One of those who listened enrapt, the well-informed and widely traveled patriarch John Adams, afterward remarked that England's Edmund Burke no longer could be rated as "the most consummate orator of modern times." Webster's speeches in Congress gave him a reputation, even among his party foes, as "the most powerful man" ever sent there from the North.

"His manner is forcible and authoritative," said William Plumer, now a Republican representative from New
Hampshire. "Nothing is left at loose ends in his state-
ments of facts or in his reasonings; and the hearer passes
from one position to another with the fullest conviction
that the result must be correct, where the steps leading to
it are so clear and obvious." During the Massachusetts
constitutional convention of 1820 one of the delegates
who was also an instructor in elocution rated Webster as
much the best speaker he had ever heard. "No man so
quickly and so thoroughly discerns a whole subject, and
elucidates it in so clear, precise, and concise a manner,"
this critic said. "His mode of speaking is peculiar; altogether unfettered by any rule, and exceedingly various."
He had "three distinct styles." The first of these, a "slow,
unimpassioned, deliberate manner," he used when he was
stating plain reasons or simple facts. The second, his "best
and most powerful," which was "slow, various, animated,"
he adopted when he was "warmed by the subject." The
third he turned to whenever he got "excited" or "impa-
tient and irritated"; then he was "very rapid; a perfect
torrent of words"; his voice loud and "on a high key; his
emphasis sharp, and almost screeching; his gestures perpetual and violent; his face alternately flushed and pale."

As he turned forty, Webster was acquiring both fame
and money, but he was yet to gain political power in
equally satisfying amounts. He was "as ambitious as Cae-
sar" and would "not be outdone by any man," a fellow
lawyer before the Supreme Court, William Wirt, observed in 1824. High tasks awaited his ambition and his
statesmanship, and in the years from 1817 to 1827 he
set himself to those demanding immediate attention. One
task was to create a legal and judicial climate favorable to

the growth of corporations, such as those of his Boston intimates, and to the development of interstate business. Another was to make a statement of conservative philosophy
which not only would express the right of property to govern but also would reconcile with it the republican dogma
of popular rule. And still another was to reorganize and
reinvigorate the Federalist party — the representative of
business interests, the vehicle of Webster's own advancement — and make it acceptable to voters at large, at least
throughout the North.

2

Corporations, when they ran against the hostility of Jef-
fersonians in the state legislatures or in Congress, found a
refuge in the Supreme Court under the arch-Federalist,
John Marshall. The great chief justice discovered in the
Constitution safeguards aplenty for vested rights, safeguards which Alexander Hamilton and others among the
Founding Fathers had intended to put there. Carrying
most of his colleagues with him, Marshall in one ringing
opinion after another aggrandized the Court as against the
Congress and the President, the national government as
against the governments of the states, and the business as
against the agricultural interest. And Webster, apparently
forgetting the state rights that had seemed so sacred to
him during the recent war, joined with Marshall in bringing out some of the nationalistic, Hamiltonian implications in the fundamental law.

In the Dartmouth College case, he scored his first great

triumph for Hamiltonian principles, and he did it as much by skillful management as by legal argument.

The case had originated in a quarrel between Dartmouth's trustees and its president, John Wheelock, son of its founder. Wheelock belonged to the Federalist party and so did the trustees, and a majority of the New Hampshire legislature as well: the dispute did not arise from differences in politics. Needing an attorney, Wheelock sent Webster a twenty-dollar retainer fee. Webster kept the money but declined to represent Wheelock when the college controversy began to divide New Hampshire along party lines, the Republicans championing the president and the Federalists, the trustees.

After winning the election of 1816, the Republicans undertook to revise Dartmouth's colonial charter so as to convert the private college into a state university. "The college was formed for the public good, not for the benefit or emolument of its trustees," declared the new governor of the state; "and the right to amend and improve acts of incorporation of this nature has been exercised by all governments." Jefferson himself, in retirement at Monticello, endorsed the governor's message as being "replete with sound principles, and truly republican." The highest court of New Hampshire, also agreeing with the governor, upheld the act of the legislature giving control of Dartmouth to the state.

Here, presented in terms of republicanism or antirepublicanism, in terms of the public interest or private rights, was a challenge to friends of the old college and to devotees of corporate property in general. Webster took up the challenge.

In his argument before the Supreme Court of the

United States, early in 1818, he followed very closely the
brief that Jeremiah Mason and a colleague had prepared
and used unsuccessfully before the New Hampshire court.
Most of the brief was inconsequential and irrelevant. The
one point that proved decisive in Marshall's mind, Webster touched upon without special emphasis and, indeed,
almost as an afterthought. What, he asked, was the meaning of the words in the Constitution: "No State shall . . .
pass any . . . law impairing the obligation of contracts"?
The Supreme Court itself, he answered, had decided in
the case of *Fletcher* v. *Peck*, involving land grants by the
State of Georgia, that "a *grant* is a contract." The Dartmouth charter, he went on, "is embraced within the very
terms of that decision," since "a grant of corporate powers
and privileges is as much a *contract* as a grant of land."

Then, after an effective pause, Webster appealed to the
emotions of the Court with an extraordinary peroration.
What he said, no one recorded at the time. Long afterward, when he was dead, a friend recalled the words and
the scene as once described by another friend who had
been there. According to this secondhand recollection,
Webster came to the touching passage: "It is, sir, as I
have said, a small college." He paused again. "And yet
there are those who love it —" His lips quivered, his eyes
filled with tears, his voice choked. And the judges in their
robes, even the strong-willed Marshall himself, sat trans-
fixed and dewy-eyed.

Doubtless they were in fact deeply moved — for the moment — but when they recovered they could arrive at no
consensus, so Marshall announced a continuation of the
case and adjourned the Court. "I have no accurate knowledge of the manner in which the judges are divided."

Webster wrote, as he tried to read their minds. "The chief and Washington, I have no doubt, are with us; *the other three holding up.* I cannot much doubt that Story will be with us *in the end,* and I think we have much more than an even chance for one of the others."

The Court was not to meet again for a year, and in the meantime Webster got busy with an educational campaign to help the hesitant or wavering members reach agreement with their chief. He had his argument printed and widely distributed, in accordance with the advice of the chief justice of Massachusetts, who told him: "Public sentiment has a great deal to do in affairs of this sort, and it ought to be well founded. That sentiment may even reach and affect a court; at least, if there be any members who wish to do right, but are a little afraid, it will be a great help to know that all the world expects they will do right." A copy of the published brief went to every important lawyer in New England and to Chancellor James Kent of New York, an imposing legal authority, who conferred with Justice William Johnson of the Federal court about the Dartmouth case. Webster sent five copies to his Supreme Court friend Justice Joseph Story, with the suggestion: "If you send one of them to each of such of the judges as you think proper, you will of course do it in the manner least likely to lead to a feeling that any indecorum has been committed by the plaintiffs."

By the time the Court reconvened, it had made up its collective mind. The New Hampshire officials, having hired the impressive William Pinkney of Baltimore as their new attorney, hoped to have the case reopened and reargued, but Marshall ignored Pinkney and calmly read his magisterial opinion. Webster then moved for, and got, an immediate judgment in favor of the Dartmouth College trustees. Before leaving the courtroom he joyfully wrote to his brother Ezekiel: "All is safe."

All was safe indeed for corporation investors fearing legislative interference with their pursuit of profits. At the moment the decision attracted little attention outside of New Hampshire and Massachusetts, but a year later the nation's leading magazine, the *North American Review,* opined that "perhaps no judicial proceedings in this country ever involved more important consequences." A principle had been proclaimed: corporation charters were contracts, and contracts were inviolable. Thereafter the states had to contend against this doctrine in their efforts to control corporate activity.

Having got a reputation as a constitutional lawyer in the Dartmouth case, Webster proceeded at once to confirm it in the case of *McCulloch* v. *Maryland.* The State of Maryland had laid a heavy tax on the Baltimore branch of the Bank of the United States. Two constitutional questions were before the Supreme Court: could Congress charter a bank and, if so, could one of the states thus tax it? As one of the bank's attorneys, Webster first repeated the arguments used originally by Hamilton to prove that the establishment of such an institution came well within the "necessary and proper" clause. Then, to dispose of the tax issue, Webster added an ingenious argument of his own. The power to tax, he said, involved a "power to destroy," and if Maryland could tax the bank at all, it could tax it to death. But the bank with its branches was an agency of the Federal government: no state could take an action tending to destroy the United States itself. In delivering the decision of the court, Marshall complimented

all the lawyers in the case for their able briefs, but he paid
Webster the additional compliment of incorporating his
very words in the majority opinion.

This verdict, however, did not quite settle the issue.
Other states, after Maryland, tried to tax the bank in one
way or another, Webster continued to represent the institution, and Marshall read successive opinions in its favor.
These and other decisions made the Supreme Court
more and more unpopular, and agitation against it came
to a head in 1824, while Webster was in Congress. To appease those demanding that the Court be curbed, he recommended that a majority of its whole membership, and
not just a majority of those actually sitting on a case, be
required to declare state laws unconstitutional. But some
of the critics of the Court were insisting on a majority of
five out of seven (the number of justices then comprising
the Court). In the nick of time Webster and Marshall
produced an argument and an opinion that pleased the
people and quieted the Congressmen.

The case of *Gibbon* v. *Ogden* involved the issue of monopoly along with that of national as against state power;
and this time both Webster and Marshall took the anti-
monopolistic side. The State of New York had granted a
steamboat company exclusive rights to carry passengers on
the Hudson River to New York City. This grant struck
neither Marshall nor Webster as sacred. Webster argued
that the constitutional power of Congress to regulate commerce between the states "must necessarily be complete,
entire and uniform." The individual states could not "assert a right of concurrent legislation" without "manifest
encroachment and confusion." Marshall agreed with
Webster. Traffic on the Hudson was opened to competi-

tion, and a local vested interest gave way to the needs of
business on a larger scale.

In this as in his other Supreme Court appearances,
Webster talked like a thoroughgoing Hamiltonian. But he
was not one. He still was unwilling to foster manufactures
by means of protective tariffs, which had occupied an important place in Hamilton's financial program.

3

The protectionist cry, renewed in 1820, came not so
much from the big business of the time as from the
smaller enterprisers, not so much from the established
manufacturing concerns as from those struggling to get a
start. It was a clamor for the sharing of economic privileges, akin to the contemporary demand for the sharing
of political power which led to the constitutional convention in Massachusetts in 1820 and to similar conventions
in other states during the next few decades. The depression following the panic of 1819 swelled the number of
the discontented and whetted their desires for more popular influence in government and more public aid to private enterprise. Replying to the restless advocates of
change, Webster in three remarkable speeches formulated
the outlines of a cogent philosophy of letting things alone.

At a meeting of Boston businessmen in Faneuil Hall
(October 2, 1820) he attacked the tariff theory so ably
that in after years, as a protectionist, he was hard put to
refute himself. In his speech of 1820 he doubted whether
tariff protection was constitutional unless it happened to

result *"incidentally* only" from duties levied "for the leading purpose of revenue." Even if permissible, he thought
such protection inadvisable because it would lead to "too
much reliance on government" and to a "perpetual contest" between the "different interests of society" as farmers and manufacturers and shipowners all lobbied for special favors in Washington. Far better to "leave men to
their own discretion" and let them "employ their capital
and labor in such occupations as they themselves found
most expedient." Only a few producers could gain from
protective duties, anyhow, and the rest of the people, as
consumers and as taxpayers, would suffer a "double loss."
Competing imports being shut out, the price of the domestic manufacture would be raised. The consumer,
therefore, must pay more for it. "And in so much as government will have lost the duty on the imported article, a
tax equal to that duty must be paid to government."

That was familiar *laissez-faire* doctrine, out of Adam
Smith, the famous Scottish economist whose *Wealth of
Nations* (1776) was an arsenal of arguments in favor of
free trade. In the rest of his speech, however, Webster
went beyond the free traders' usual stand and seemed not
so much to echo Adam Smith as to anticipate Karl Marx,
though in fact he was restating ideas familiar enough
among the old Federalists of New England such as John
Adams. Webster said he was not "advancing any agrarian
notions," any revolutionary ideas, but he thought "those
employments which tended to make the poor both more
numerous and more poor, and the rich less in number,
but perhaps more rich, were not employments for us to
encourage by taxing other employments." And this he believed would be "the tendency of the manufacturing sys-

tem pushed to excess," for "manufacturing capital came
in the end to be owned but by few."

He preferred agriculture to manufacturing because, he
said, agriculture was more conducive to "individual respectability and happiness" and to social well-being also.
Let Europe keep its workshops: the United States was and
should remain a country predominantly of farmers tilling
their own acres. Such was the happy condition of this
country, and such the low value of land, that almost every
industrious laborer had the means, by his labor, of becoming in a short time a freeholder. "He thereby obtains a
feeling of respectability, a sense of propriety and of personal independence which is generally essential to ele-
vated character. He has a stake in society, and is inclined,
therefore, rather to uphold than to demolish it." The reverse was true of the factory hands in Europe. "They have
no stake in society; they hang loose upon it, and are often
neither happy in their condition nor without danger to
the state."

As for the argument that factories gave jobs to women
and to children, even those of tender years, it was "no
recommendation" of protective tariffs to Webster. He
thought manufactures "a kind of employment not suited
to the one or the other," to women or to children.

Having thus disposed of protectionism and industrialism as threats to society and the state, Webster several
weeks later (December 15, 1820) in the Massachusetts
constitutional convention, turned to repelling another
threat, that of rule by mere majorities. The convention, in
which he starred among the conservatives, including some
of the most illustrious men of Massachusetts history,
"generally was well disposed," he thought, but "there was

a good deal of inflammable matter and some radicalism in it." The more inflammable and radical members complained that, under the old constitution, the rich were better represented than the poor, at least in the state senate, where the number of representatives from each district depended not on the number of its people but on the amount of its taxable wealth. The reformers pressed an amendment apportioning senators according to population alone. Though Webster spoke eloquently against the change, he could not prevent it.

But he could and did present a thoughtful, realistic disquisition on the relation of property to government (on which his fellow delegate, John Adams, had expounded years before). He ranged widely over the literature of politics, from antiquity to recent times, citing Aristotle, Grotius, Montesquieu, Francis Bacon, Walter Raleigh, and above all James Harrington, whose seventeenth-century classic *The Commonwealth of Oceana* went to prove "that power *naturally* and *necessarily* follows property." With this, Webster wholeheartedly agreed. "Not, indeed, that every man's power should be in exact proportion to his property, but that, in a general sense, and in a general form, property as such should have its weight and influence in political arrangement." To give property due weight and influence, the American Revolution had been fought: a conservative Revolution "undertaken not to shake or plunder property, but to protect it."

Just one week after offering this theory to his fellow delegates in Boston, Webster restated and extended it in his bicentennial oration at Plymouth (December 22, 1820). He now attempted to show that in the United States property rule and popular government were one

and the same. The American government, he said, had
been so constructed "as to give to all, or at least to a very
great majority, an interest in its preservation; to found it,
as other things are founded, on men's interest." It was
stable because those who desired its continuance, those
with property, were more numerous and more powerful
than those who desired its dissolution, those without property. Power, of course, was not always to be measured by
mere numbers. Education, wealth, talents, all were elements of power; but numbers were "ordinarily the most
important consideration."

The freest possible government "would not be long
acceptable" if the laws created a "rapid accumulation of
property in few hands" and rendered the great mass of
the population penniless. In such a case "the popular
power would be likely to break in upon the rights of
property," or else the influence of property would be
likely to "limit and control the exercise of popular power."
Thus universal suffrage could not long exist in a community where there was great inequality of ownership.
The propertyless would oppose "laws made for the protection of property." Were this class to become numerous,
it would look "on property as its prey and plunder" and
be "ready, at all times, for violence and revolution."

No wonder that the Webster of 1820 opposed protective tariffs, believing as he did that they would multiply
this dangerous proletariat.

4

In Congress, in 1824, Webster met the irrepressible tariff advocates again and did battle with their greatest champion, the tall, magnetic speaker of the House, Henry Clay. Protection was a part of Clay's national economic plan, which as before embraced also the United States Bank and a Federal network of roads and waterways. He now put it forth under the appealing name of the "American system." His new tariff bill contained something for important interests in several states: hemp producers in his own Kentucky, lead miners in Missouri and Illinois, ironmakers in Pennsylvania, wool growers in Ohio and New York, and cotton and woolen manufacturers in Rhode Island and Massachusetts. All desired higher duties — with one very notable exception.

The largest textile firm in the country, the Boston Manufacturing Company, with its efficient mills at Waltham and Lowell, did not need protection for itself and did not want it for potential competitors. Nor did the shipbuilders and shipowners of Boston favor duties on iron and hemp or on other products which would increase the cost of ships and keep out the imports that entered into the carrying trade.

Before speaking out, Webster took pains to learn the opinions of Boston businessmen. As soon as the tariff bill was printed, he sent copies to fifty of his most important constituents and asked for their detailed comments. Thus he informed and fortified himself for the debate.

Taking the floor, he first refuted Clay's contention that

the tariff was an "American" policy and free trade hence an un-American one. "Sir," he said, "that is the truest American policy which shall most usefully employ American capital and American labor, and best sustain the whole population. With me it is a fundamental axiom, it is interwoven with all my opinions, that the great interests of the country are united and inseparable; that agriculture, commerce, and manufactures will prosper together or languish together; and that all legislation is dangerous which proposes to benefit one of these without looking to consequences which may fall on the others."

Having begun strongly, on the high plane of principle, Webster weakened his case when he descended to details and began to make exceptions. He was dealing with the measure, he explained, "not as a whole, for it has no entire and homogeneous character, but as a collection of different enactments, some of which meet my approbation and some of which do not." He did not object to protection for woolen cloths, for example. "But then this bill proposes, also, a very high duty upon imported wool."

Though he secured some modifications in the bill, he could not prevent its passage. And the concessions he made for the benefit of some of his constituents were fatal to his whole position. He was no longer standing on principle: he was poised to represent, as precisely as he could, the balance of contending interests at home. When that balance should swing to the protectionist side, so would he.

5

The Federalists still had Marshall on the Supreme Court, and here and there they could send a man like Webster to Congress, but they had ceased to be a national party by 1820. They did not even put up a presidential candidate that year, and James Monroe gained a second term with all the electoral votes except one. Though his re-election was hailed as beginning an "Era of Good Feeling," the time was actually one of economic discontent, sectional bitterness, factional quarrels, and political feelings rather more bad than good. In the nation as a whole, the two-party system having broken down, politics became a free-for-all among individual leaders, each trying to find attractive issues for a new and broad-based organization.

To this pursuit Webster himself devoted considerable effort. For the uses of politics, he needed a platform with popular appeal. So long as Boston disapproved the tariff, he could hardly take up Clay's American system, despite its lures of profit for influential groups in various parts of the country. He could, however, experiment with programs less definite and less divisive, with crusades for humanity, morality, and liberty either at home or abroad.

When, in 1819, people North and South got excited over the question of whether Missouri should join the Union as a free or a slave state, he rose to the occasion by declaring to a public meeting of Bostonians that the time had come to place "a barrier to the further progress of slavery," lest it "roll on desolating the vast expanse of the continent to the Pacific Ocean." In that kind of opposition

to the Missouri Compromise, some wiseacres saw a scheme
of old Federalists to win new converts on an antislavery
platform, but the crisis passed without political benefit to
Webster or his friends.

Another opportunity came a few years later when, in
the faraway Balkans, the Greeks rose in revolt against the
Ottoman Empire. Friends of the fighting Hellenes got
busy in the United States. They denounced the atrocities
of the Turks (who, it was said, gathered human ears by
the bushel), collected money for the revolutionists, and
petitioned Congress to do what it could for Greek independence. The Hellenic enthusiasm in this country
reached its climax at the beginning of 1824, an election
year.

Then, primed by his good friend Edward Everett, foremost of American Philhellenists, Webster in Congress
brought his massive oratory to bear in favor of the Greeks.
Their cause, he said, was ours. It was civilization against
the brute, liberty against the cruel oppressor, Christianity
against the infidel, international law against the lawless.
It was a world-wide issue, with the Holy Alliance and all
the reactionary forces of Europe on the side of the scarcely
human Turk. "Does it not become us, then, is it not a
duty imposed on us," Webster asked, "to give our weight
to the side of liberty and justice, to let mankind know
that we are not tired of our own institutions, and to protest
against the asserted power of altering at pleasure the law
of the civilized world?" Not that we should go to war or
even risk involvement in hostilities. Not at all. Our moral
support would be enough. "Moral causes come into consideration, in proportion as the progress of knowledge is advanced; and the public opinion of the civilized world is

rapidly gaining an ascendancy over mere brutal force."

On the face of it this should have been a safe stand as well as a popular one, this proposal to quell the forces of reaction throughout the world by means of a congressional resolution. But it made trouble for Webster.

His own Boston merchants did not relish the possibility, however remote, of trouble with the Ottoman Empire, which allowed a profitable trade at the port of Smyrna. The opium crop alone was worth a million dollars a year, and more than half of it was carried away in American ships. "This is no small item," Thomas H. Perkins wrote, under the pseudonym of "A Merchant," in a Boston newspaper. "Shall we then go on a crusade in favor of the Greeks and hazard the liberty of our citizens and a valuable trade?" In answer, a couple of Webster's Massachusetts colleagues in the House argued that an independent Greece would provide much greater trading opportunities than the single port of Smyrna, but the merchants remained unconvinced.

So did Monroe's Secretary of State, John Quincy Adams, who viewed Webster's resolve as a device calculated to embarrass him and the Monroe administration. Adams steered the administration men in Congress against Webster, and they soon killed his resolution with an indefinite postponement. Some of the Philhellenes thought it might have fared better if someone other than a New Englander and a Federalist had sponsored it.

6

In the election of 1824 none of the several candidates got a majority in the electoral college, so the House of Representatives had to pick a President from among the three highest. Actually the choice lay between only two, John Quincy Adams and Andrew Jackson. To which of them should Webster and his Federalist friends give their votes?

For a while he remained undecided, coy. The Federalists looked upon Adams as a renegade who had deserted to Jefferson at the time of the embargo. Some of them considered Jackson a lesser evil, and Webster himself at first thought the general very "presidential" in appearance, "grave, mild, and reserved." During the Christmas vacation, though, Webster visited Madison and Jefferson at their Virginia homes and revised his opinion of Jackson (and of Madison and Jefferson as well). He found Jefferson thoroughly alarmed at the prospect of a President like Jackson — a mere military chieftain, a person of terrible passions and rages, altogether a dangerous man. After returning to Washington, Webster secured from Adams a pledge not to discriminate against Federalists in awarding government jobs, then came out for him.

Clay, not Webster, did most to make Adams President, but Webster co-operated. When the day came, early in 1825, for the balloting in the House (each state casting one vote), half of the states were ready, thanks to Clay, to give their votes to Adams. One more vote was needed, and the New York delegation was evenly divided. Clay and Webster went to work to change the mind of one of its members, Stephen Van Rensselaer, "the Patroon." They cornered the wealthy dotard and scared him with talk of the dire consequences to follow for men of property if Jackson were elected. In confusion, the old Patroon bowed his head to pray, saw an Adams ballot on the floor, accepted it as a sign, and stuffed it into the ballot box.

With Adams inaugurated, Webster for the first time belonged to a group in control of the presidency. At first he hoped to see the administration broadly based on all factions, with his own Federalists as a nucleus, and so he recommended that the patronage be dispensed without regard to old party alignments. Further to dispel the factional spirit, he preached a gospel of Americanism whenever he had an audience.

On Bunker Hill, on a June day in 1825, tens of thousands thrilled when, in the midst of his oration commemorating the famous battle, he suddenly addressed the Revolutionary veterans on the slope before him: "VENERABLE MEN!" But his theme was more the American future than the American past. Upon the success of the political experiment in the United States, he averred, would depend the fate of popular government throughout the earth. "The last hopes of mankind, therefore, rest with us" — with our Union. "Let us cultivate a true spirit of union and harmony," he concluded. "Let us act under a settled conviction, and an habitual feeling, that these twenty-four States are one country."

An even more dramatic occasion for Webster's oratory arrived the next year when, on the fiftieth anniversary of the Declaration of Independence, two of its authors, Jefferson and John Adams, died within a few hours of one another. In his discourse on the lives of the two men Webster gave much the more attention to the Massachusetts Federalist, but he praised the Virginia Republican generously too, and he refrained from invidious comparisons of their careers or political principles. "With America, and in America, a new era commences in human affairs," he announced in his peroration, turning once more from things gone by to things ahead. "America, America, our country, fellow-citizens, our own dear and native land . . ."

These appeals to patriotism — sincere enough, no doubt — failed to charm away the party spirit. Adams having named Clay as his Secretary of State, the thwarted Jacksonians raised the cry of "corrupt bargain" and at once began a campaign to elect the hero of New Orleans in 1828, making a partisan issue of everything that Adams tried to do. In the House, loyally defending the administration, Webster was unable to salvage any of its frustrated plans. Federal jobholders, even highly placed ones, were conniving with the foe. Against them Webster and Clay pleaded with Adams to use the patronage ruthlessly but the stubborn puritan refused to do it. Webster could not even get the position he coveted for himself — that of minister to England.

To form the kind of new party he desired, he would need more than patriotic flights of eloquence, more even than government jobs. By 1827 he was ready for the advice that Clay then offered him. This concerned a new political alliance, to be based on the American system, promising government aid to the dominant groups in both New England and the West.

I I I
Words Are Things
1827–1833

"Was it Mirabeau who has told us that words are things? They are indeed things, and things of mighty influence."

HE WAS Senator Webster now, in 1827. Within the next six years he was to win the brightest of all his honors in the never-ending tourney of political debate. But the mother of his children — the wife who had encouraged and, from a distance, applauded his preliminary successes — was not to share the glory yet to come.

During the one winter that Mrs. Webster had spent with her husband in Washington, she seldom forgot the four children she had left at home, especially the baby Charles, not yet two. "I am glad to hear that little Charley pities the Greeks and intends giving them plum pudding," she wrote during the Philhellenic craze to Daniel Fletcher, who was the oldest of the children now that Grace, the firstborn, was dead.

The next winter, when little Charley himself was dying, she tried to keep the news of his illness from his father, the busy statesman, then planning his visit to thr residence of Thomas Jefferson. "I cannot tell you how much I regret that the unpleasant intelligence reached you before you had set out for Monticello," she wrote from Boston; "if you had got away before, you might have enjoyed the excursion." Lonely and troubled after the baby's death, she poured out her feelings in letter after letter to her husband during the long absences when he was preoccupied with affairs of state:

"My poor old thimble! I did not know what had become of it. I value it only as being a purchase I made when I lived in Portsmouth; ere the 'blight of sorrow had ever come o'er me.' You were with us here so short a time my Love, I fear you can hardly see us in your mind's eye."

"I have felt very much interested in the great affairs at W., but I doubt if I ever go there again. Our children, if they live, will require my constant care — more than I could bestow in such a place — and if it must be so, if your duty calls you there, I must submit — it is doubtless best it should be so."

"In my sleep last night you were with us — but I awoke and the delightful vision fled!"

"I, who never stir from my own fireside but to enter a Church, can have nothing to communicate but the health or sickness of my family, as it pleases Providence — the shining of the glorious sun, or the howling of the storm."

"It is mortifying to reflect how much I am behind you in everything. I know no one respects but rather despises those they consider very much their inferiors."

"I would not forget that Mrs. Tickner desired me to mention her particularly to you. When you compare her letters with mine, my dear Husband, I am well aware that the difference in length will be the most trifling. You must have the mortification to reflect that Mrs. T. is the daughter of a man of *millions,* and has enjoyed, since her infancy, every advantage which wealth can bestow, while your wife is the daughter of a poor country clergyman — all the early part of her life passed in obscurity, toiling with hands not *'fair'* for subsistence. These are humiliating truths, which I regret more on your account than any other."

At last Grace Webster started for Washington again with her husband, the new senator, but she got no farther than New York. There, with a tumor too deep for surgery, she lingered for a while, then died in January, 1828. At her funeral in Boston Webster refused to ride in a carriage. Despite his rheumatism and a severe cold, he took a child in each hand and, bareheaded, trudged after the hearse through mist and slush to the grave.

Not quite two years after that, at forty-seven, he married again. His bride, Caroline LeRoy, only thirty-one, was the daughter of a New York merchant who had retired with a fortune. Sociable and vivacious, she was never to be held down by children of her own and, though a kindly and conscientious stepmother, she had ample time for companionship with Webster. Even when apart from him, she was not given to moping, not even on that New Year's Day when, all alone in Boston, she expected visitors to call informally, as in New York, and had her table "spread with cakes liquor & wine" but had "not a soul to take them." She filled her cheerful letters from New York with the gossip of society, with political opinions of leading merchants, with assurances of her love. And Webster, always gallant, sent her in return such tokens as the magnolia blossom he picked one May day in Washington. After more than a dozen years of marriage to her, he wrote to another woman, the wife of a friend: "If you, who always thought her a great beauty, were to see her now, you would agree that she had still further improved."

The second Mrs. Webster was less inclined than the first to restrain his propensities for high living and careless spending. He came more and more to crave money, as an addict craves the drug, and he was to satisfy that craving in ways that eventually hurt his reputation. For the moment, though, he stood forth as the superb orator of his time, the Defender of the Constitution, the white knight of the Union. And his lady, glorying in his glory, cheered him on but cautioned: "I only entreat of you to *keep cool* & not subject yourself to attack from those *hot headed* nullifiers."

2

What aroused the nullifiers and tried the Union was the tariff of 1828. By that time the sections had realigned themselves on the protectionism issue. The Middle states of New York, New Jersey, and Pennsylvania had always favored the protective tariff and still favored it. The Western states were coming around to it. But the South, abandoning plans for the development of textile mills, and depending more and more on the export of the cotton crop, now demanded free trade. And New England, once reluctant to try protection, was at last predominantly for it.

The woolen manufacturers of Massachusetts and Rhode Island complained that the law of 1824 had become inadequate when the British government advantaged their competitors by removing most of its duty on raw wool. The British, it was said, were dumping woolens on the American market at prices that stopped half the textile machinery of New England. Petitioning Congress, the distressed millowners expected relief from the woolens bill of 1827. Now, for the first time, Congressman Webster voted for a tariff measure. It passed the House but was defeated in the Senate when Vice President Calhoun cast his negative vote to break a tie.

Thus frustrated, the protectionists of New England and the Middle and Western states combined to bring pressure upon Congress, after getting together in a grand tariff convention at Harrisburg, where Webster's brother Ezekiel and his friend Abbott Lawrence represented New Hampshire and Massachusetts. But some of the Boston shipowners continued to resist, among them Henry Lee, who authored a fat pamphlet in which he restated the doctrines of free trade and denounced Webster for his inconsistency in voting for the woolens bill.

In the Senate, in 1828, Webster faced a dilemma when a much more inclusive bill, incorporating the demands of protectionists in several states, came up from the House. This measure contained a high woolens duty, as his constituents desired, but it contained others which they could not stand — high duties on flax, hemp, iron, lead, molasses, and raw wool. And, as if these were not bad enough, Senator Thomas Hart Benton of Missouri called for a still higher molasses tax, an outright prohibition on the importation of raw wool, and a tariff on oranges, lemons, and limes, "to protect the products of Florida," as he said. But Webster's woolen manufacturers wanted cheap raw material, of course, and his importing merchants cheap shipbuilding supplies as well as cheap molasses and fruit, essential items in Boston's overseas trade. Webster tried to dispose of his dilemma by eliminating the objectionable duties already in the bill and preventing the addition of new and even worse ones.

In his exasperation he accused the South and the West of vindictiveness toward New England, saying of the molasses duty in particular: ". . . the tax is to be left in the bill, that New England may be made *to feel.*" This hateful animus had been stirred up in other sections, he charged, by a "loud and ceaseless cry" against what was called "the cupidity, the avarice, the monopolizing spirit of New England manufacturers." He then implied and others later said that the bill had taken its shape from a Jacksonian plot to embarrass New Englanders and discredit their President, John Quincy Adams. Doubtless some politicians did see it as an electioneering device, but others intended it seriously as a means of benefiting the farmers and manufacturers of the Middle states and the West. The issue lay not only between Jacksonians and Adamsites, and not only between free-traders and protectionists, but also between advocates of protection for different and conflicting interests. What was reasonable to one tariffite was "abominable" to another.

Southerners voted against reductions in the hope that

the bill, intact, would so antagonize New Englanders that they would help defeat it. Webster could not escape a most difficult choice. His Massachusetts colleague in the Senate refused all along to approve the bill, and many of the Massachusetts representatives in the House remained uncertain which way to vote. On the final ballot Webster went for the tariff, wool and molasses duties and all. He carried with him enough New England votes to pass the bill.

It was a decision hard to make and hard to rationalize, but Webster did not lack for explanations, then or afterward. The tariff of 1824, he argued, had fixed the policy of the United States. Having failed to defeat it, his constituents gave in to the majority will. They took their money out of shipping and put it into woolen and other manufactures under the protection and encouragement of the law. So they had a right to expect continuing protection for their investments, he declared. As for his earlier constitutional doubts, these had assumed that the tariff should be based on the congressional power to tax. Now his doubts had disappeared, had been dispersed by a recent publication of James Madison, the Father of the Constitution himself, who indicated that protection of industry was a proper exercise of the congressional power to regulate commerce.

To those of his constituents on whose enterprises the new tariff bore "with great severity," Webster said that the blow had fallen "almost as powerfully and heavily" on him as on them. He regretted having had to differ with his Massachusetts colleague in the Senate. "The only difference," he said, "was, when the measure had assumed its final shape, whether the good it contained so far pre-

ponderated over its acknowledged evil, as to justify the
reception and support of the whole together." But on some
subjects he had "had the good fortune to act in perfect
unison" with the other senator and with every representative of the state. Like them, he had voted to give generous pensions to veterans of the Revolutionary War. He
had also voted for Federal expenditures to improve rivers
and harbors. "The breakwater in the Delaware, useful to
Philadelphia, is useful also to all the shipowners in the
United States," he pointed out. "If the mouths of the
Southern rivers be deepened and improved, the neighboring cities are benefited, but so also are the ships which
visit them; and if the Mississippi and Ohio be rendered
more safe for navigation, the great markets of consump-
tion along their shores are the more readily and cheaply
approached by the products of the factories and fisheries
of New England." So, with internal improvements, he
sought to mollify those Boston businessmen who still held
out against the protective tariff.

Few of them held out much longer. Though the merchants had lost their trade in India cottons and English
woolens, they still could import fruits and wines, Chinese
teas and bric-a-brac, and other exotic products which remained almost duty-free. They could also profit from new
trades that grew with the growth of tariff-protected manufactures: wool from South American ports, coal from Philadelphia, cotton from New Orleans and Charleston; and
cheap textiles to China and to other markets of the world.
And they could and did continue to invest their surplus
profits in textile mills. Thus, by 1831, Boston had become
so thoroughly protectionist that, in a congressional election, the manufacturer and tariff propagandist Nathan Ap-

pleton decisively defeated the India merchant and free-
trade pamphleteer Henry Lee. With protectionism now
the orthodox dogma at home, Webster could preach it
without qualification and without fear.

3

For John C. Calhoun, in South Carolina, the case was
just the opposite. While Massachusetts merchants prospered, the South Carolina planters were losing money.
Their state was stagnating, its population increasing little
if at all, its countryside showing signs of ruin and decay.
The South Carolinians could have found reasons for their
plight in their one-crop, slave economy and their worn-out
soil, on which they could hardly raise cotton in successful
competition with planters on the rich lands of the new
Southwest. But they blamed their troubles on the "tariff
of abominations" alone. Some of them threatened to escape the hateful law by revolution, by secession. Here was
a challenge Calhoun must meet if he was to maintain his
leadership in the state and make a future for himself in
national politics.

Quietly, on his upcountry plantation, during the summer after the enactment of the abominations bill, he wrote
out a rationale for possible action by his state. He was
finding a way for his aggrieved constituents to evade, by
constitutional rather than revolutionary means, the consequences of the protectionist policy he had done as much as
anyone to fix upon the nation a dozen years before. Out of
the Constitution, which he then had said was not a thing

for logicians to exercise their ingenuity upon, he was spinning fine webs of logic in which to enmesh the latter-day
tariffites.

He started his reasoning with the assumption that sov-
ereignty, the ultimate source of power, lay in the states
considered as separate political communities. He went on
to assume that these separate peoples, through their ratifying conventions, had authorized the Constitution and the
Federal government. Putting this in legal terminology, he
described the states (meaning their peoples, not their
governments) as the "principals," the Federal government as their "agent," and the Constitution as a "compact" containing instructions within which the agent was
to operate.

From these assumptions the rest of his theory followed
logically enough. The Supreme Court was not competent
to judge whether acts of Congress were constitutional
since the Court, like the Congress, was only a branch of an
agency created by the states. No, Calhoun reasoned, the
principals must decide, each for itself, whether their instructions were violated. If Congress enacted a law of
doubtful constitutionality — say, a protective tariff — the
people of any state could elect a convention, and if the
delegates decided that Congress had gone too far, they
could declare the Federal law null and void within their
state. In that state the law would remain inoperative until
three fourths of the whole number of states should ratify
an amendment to the Constitution specifically assigning
Congress the power in question. And if the other states
should ever get around to doing this, the nullifying state
would then submit — or it could secede.

But Calhoun thought of nullification as an alternative

and not a preliminary to secession. To him it was a "conservative principle," one tending to conserve and not to destroy the Union. It required agreement on Federal policy not only from the people of the nation as a whole — the "numerical" or "absolute" majority — but also from the peoples of the individual states — the "concurrent" majorities. The right of state veto, the need for unanimity, would in itself make Northern businessmen and Southern planters regardful of one another's interests. Or so Calhoun professed to believe.

The legislature of South Carolina published his first statement of the nullification theory, in 1828, in a document entitled *The South Carolina Exposition and Protest*. This denounced the tariff of abominations as unconstitutional, unfair, and unendurable — a law fit to be nullified. The protest did not bear Calhoun's name. He had good reason for anonymity: he was the Vice President of the United States, under Adams, and was running for re-election on the Jackson ticket.

In the campaign of 1828 there were again two parties, the Democratic Republicans for Jackson, the National Republicans for Adams. The Adams organization in Massachusetts had been formed the previous year by men of both Republican and Federalist antecedents. They met in Boston to combine against the radicals who agitated for a free bridge across the Charles River in disregard of the property rights of a company to which the state had granted a toll-bridge monopoly. For the governorship, to succeed himself, the conservatives nominated an ex-Republican, Levi Lincoln. For the United States Senate, they nominated the ex-Federalist Daniel Webster (who was elected in 1827).

Not all the old Massachusetts Federalists became National Republicans. Some joined the Jackson party, and they campaigned with special bitterness against Adams, the renegade who years before had deserted to support Jefferson and the embargo. Nettled, Adams accused them of having plotted high treason at that time, when there was talk of taking New England out of the Union. In reply their Boston paper, the *Jackson Republican,* intimated that if the Jackson Federalists ever had toyed with traitorous ideas, so had the Adams Federalists, and Webster in particular. The Jacksonian propaganda failed in Massachusetts, Adams carrying every county, though running far behind Jackson in the country as a whole.

After the election Webster could have dismissed the treason insinuation as campaign oratory, which it was, but he chose to treat it as a personal affront. He kept on with a suit for criminal libel against the *Jackson Republican* editor, a henchman of Calhoun's. At the trial the editor's counsel contended that the paper, in implicating Webster in secessionist schemes, had not thereby imputed to him any treasonable designs. "The several states are independent and not dependent," the defense maintained. "Every state has a right to secede from the Union without committing treason." As authority for this extreme interpretation of the rights of states, the defense shrewdly offered two of Webster's own productions, his pamphlet on the embargo laws (1808) and the Rockingham Memorial (1812). With such evidence and argument before them, the jurymen could not agree among themselves that the editor had defamed Webster.

The trial gave publicity to old notions of state rights at the very moment when Calhoun, anonymously, was reviv-

ing them in his more sophisticated form. Once inaugurated, he waited to see what would happen to the tariff
and to the spirit of revolt at home before he came out
openly for nullification. Within a year, one of his South
Carolina followers championed his new philosophy in the
Senate, over which he presided. Eventually he led his
state to put the theory into practice, then appeared himself in the Senate to expound the ingenious logic of state
rights. Against the disciple and then against the master,
both latecomers to the particularist view, a near-nullifica-
tionist of earlier years strode forward to deliver for the
cause of national supremacy some blows so mighty that
they still resound.

4

The Webster-Hayne debate, in January 1830, grew out
of a Senate discussion of public lands, provoked when a
senator from Connecticut suggested stopping all surveys
and sales for a time. In this proposal the rugged Jacksonian from Missouri, Thomas Hart Benton, thought he saw
a new move in an old conspiracy of New England against
the West. Now, he thundered, the Yankees, while aiming
to keep workers at home and wages down, were also
scheming to choke off the growth and prosperity of the
frontier. Taking up where Benton left off, the debonair
senator from South Carolina, Robert Y. Hayne, offered
sympathy and support to the West on behalf of the South.
He hinted that the West and the South might combine in
self-defense on a platform of low land prices and low

tariff rates. Here was a threat to the interests of the men in the countinghouses along Boston's State Street.

Their Senator Webster, busy with a Supreme Court case, happened by the Senate chamber while Hayne was in the midst of his speech. He went in to listen. Next day he took the floor, ready with words by which to keep South and West apart and save the interests of his own constituents. Ignoring Benton, he directed his remarks to Hayne and, through him, to Calhoun in the Vice President's chair. He reviewed much of the history of the republic, with occasional disregard for historical facts, to prove that New England had always been the friend of the West. Recalling the tariff of 1816, he also exonerated New England from blame, if blame there was, for starting the protectionist policy. Then he changed the subject and spoke gravely of disunionists and disunionism in South Carolina.

Thus he challenged Hayne to meet him, not on the original ground of the tariff and the public lands, but on the issue of state rights versus national power, an issue that could be made to seem one of treason versus patriotism. And in due time Hayne came back with a flashing defense of South Carolina doctrines while Calhoun in his chair looked down with occasional nods and smiles of approval, and Webster in his seat took notes, leaned back in thought, or grunted in audible dissent.

It took Webster two afternoons to deliver what schoolboys were afterward to know as the second reply to Hayne. The crowd in the gallery and on the floor, including many gaily bonneted ladies, expected a fine performance in the country's greatest show, the Senate forum, and they were not disappointed: Webster was at his eloquent best. With infinite variety, now calm and factual, now electric with emotion, he held his audience hour after hour, sometimes sending shivers through the crowd, as when he shook his finger at the Vice President and spoke directly to him in a cavernous, rumbling voice.

In justifying his own record and that of his state and section, Webster conceded nothing. He denied that he or any of his old Federalist friends had ever said or done anything to make a precedent for the South Carolina nullifiers. Hayne having quoted his 1824 speech against protection, he again threw back Calhoun's 1816 arguments in favor of it. He asserted that his own and New England's opinions on the subject, rightly understood, had always been perfectly consistent.

"I go for the Constitution as it is, and for the Union as it is," he declaimed, as he turned finally to an exposition of the "true principles" of the Constitution. "It is, Sir, the people's Constitution, the people's government, made for the people, made by the people, and answerable to the people." And he meant one people, the whole nation. He concluded with the ringing appeal: "Liberty *and* Union, now and for ever, one and inseparable!"

He was speaking not only to the Senate and the gallery but also to the nation at large. Though he called his speech "in the strictest sense unexpected," it was anything but impromptu, for its ideas had been developing in his mind for years. Long since, with Marshall's co-operation, he had made the doctrine of national power prevail before the Supreme Court, and now he was going to educate the public. Before allowing the speech to be published, he spent almost a month revising the stenographic report of it. Within the next few months the public printers Gales and Seaton distributed forty thousand copies, and from other presses at least twenty different editions soon appeared. Never before had a speech in Congress been so widely read.

Never had one been so enthusiastically acclaimed, or its author so highly honored. "Mr. Webster never stood so high in this country as at this moment," thought Amos Lawrence, the Boston merchant, "and I doubt if there be any man, either in Europe or America, his superior." Lawrence proffered and Webster modestly accepted a handsome and expensive silver service fittingly inscribed to the Defender of the Constitution.

A group of New York businessmen thanked him with a public dinner, and in his remarks to them Webster recognized that they felt a more than merely sentimental attachment to the Union ("as it is") and the Constitution ("as it is"). "Without national character, without public credit, without systematic finance, without uniformity of commercial laws, all other advantages possessed by this city would have decayed and perished, like unripe fruit," he reminded the New Yorkers. "To speak of arresting the laws of the Union, of interposing state power in matters of commerce and revenue, of weakening the full and just authority of the general government, would be, in regard to this city, but another mode of speaking of commercial ruin, of abandoned wharfs, of vacated houses, of diminished and dispersing population, of bankrupt merchants, of mechanics without employment, and laborers without bread."

But Webster gained applause not only in New England and New York, and not only from those who stood to profit directly from the endorsement of his constitutional views. The Virginia planter and former President, James Madison, returned his thanks and his praise for the "very powerful speech" after Webster thoughtfully sent him a copy. "It crushes 'nullification,'" wrote Madison, "and must hasten an abandonment of secession." Everywhere, even in the South, the speech resonated in the minds of unionists, playing upon a sense of common nationality which had been growing stronger year by year since the War of 1812. Of all American statesmen, Webster had "succeeded in riveting most strongly the attention of the whole Union," said Thomas Hamilton, a British traveler who visited the United States soon after the great reply to Hayne. "From the Gulf of St. Lawrence to that of Mexico, from Cape Sable to Lake Superior, his name has become, as it were, a household word."

Though the National Republicans cheered him the loudest, many Jacksonians added their applause. With his appeal to patriotism he not only headed off the threatened rapprochement of South and West on the platform of free trade and cheap land — and state rights. He also opened a rift between West and South within the Democratic Republican party, a rift that was to widen with the estrangement of Jackson and Calhoun. When the South Carolina nullifiers finally prepared to act, Calhoun was caught in a dilemma: he had to take the lead in nullification, with all its risks, or lose his standing in state politics. Webster, with most of the country behind him, faced no such worrisome choice. For him, the unionist role was now the one to play.

5

After waiting four years for Congress to remove the "abominations" from the tariff, the South Carolina followers of Calhoun had little patience left, and they lost that little when Congress denied them any real relief in the tariff of 1832. Few of the New England tariffites were willing to concede a thing. John Quincy Adams, once the President, now a Congressman, tried to persuade Webster to accept a reduction of duties in general and a repeal of the duty on raw wool in particular. But Webster — and New England — had changed so much since 1828 that now he would not even give up the wool tariff. "He said, no, he could not do that," Adams recorded; "it had prodigiously increased the breed of sheep, and the repeal of it would be very unpopular in New England." The wool growers of New England must not be hurt, no matter how loudly the cotton growers of South Carolina might complain.

Complaint gave way to action in the fall of 1832 when the nullifiers, overriding the opposition of the unionist minority in South Carolina, called a convention and declared both of the latest tariff acts null and void, then in the legislature passed laws to prevent the collection of duties within the state. According to Calhoun's theory all this was strictly constitutional, and the people in the rest of the states had no rightful recourse except to amend the Constitution — or repeal the tariff. But the people of other states failed to react as his theory supposed they would.

In the White House, Jackson proclaimed officially that nullifiers were traitors and threatened unofficially to hang the arch-nullifier Calhoun. In Congress, during the winter of 1832-1833, the administration leaders proposed to coerce the nullifiers with a "force bill" providing for using the Army and the Navy to see that duties were collected in South Carolina, and at the same time offered to conciliate them with the Verplanck bill, reducing the tariff. In the Senate the opposition leader Henry Clay introduced a competing plan for compromise which excluded force and provided for a gradual reduction of tariff rates. Jackson himself, insisting on coercion, refused at first to hear of concessions of any kind until South Carolina conformed to Federal law. For Webster, the choice lay between Jackson's stand and that of Clay.

In the late presidential campaign — Clay against Jackson — Webster had endorsed wholeheartedly Clay's candidacy and his economic program, including his new proposal for distributing among all the states the proceeds from the sales of public land. And he had condemned the warlike proclivities of Jackson, even as applied to a nullification attempt, which was anticipated. "We are told that the President will immediately employ the military force and blockade Charleston!" he had exclaimed on the stump. "For one, I raise my voice beforehand against the unauthorized employment of military power, and against suspending the authority of the laws, by an armed force, under the pretence of putting down nullification." The President must not act until Congress specifically had authorized him to do so, Webster said.

Changing his tune, he parted from Clay and sided with Jackson when, a few weeks later, the crisis actually came.

At news of the President's proclamation against the nullifiers, when he was about to leave Boston for the opening of Congress, he delayed long enough to attend a Union meeting in Faneuil Hall. "I shall give the President my entire and cordial support," he announced. "If the government, on this first trial, shall be found not able to keep all the states in their proper places, from that moment the whole Union is virtually dissolved." In the Senate he pressed the issue against the nullifiers by advocating the force bill and resisting both schemes of tariff reduction. He agreed more nearly with Jackson than did some of Jackson's own partisans in Congress. One of them contemned Webster as a politician more interested in winning debates than in saving the Union, and another, sarcastic about Webster's "fire and brimstone," believed that the real friends of the President looked for compromise, not force. Though likewise critical of Webster, Clay's followers did not quite agree with the conciliatory men among the Jacksonians, since Clay desired credit for himself as the great compromiser. As Webster aligned himself with Jackson, so Clay drew together with Calhoun.

Having resigned the vice presidency, participated in the nullification proceedings, and received a Senate appointment from the South Carolina governor (now Hayne), Calhoun braved the threats of Jackson and returned to Washington early in 1833 to defend his theory and its practice personally on the Senate floor. He introduced a set of resolutions on the "constitutional compact" and made a speech against the force bill.

Webster's reply to Calhoun, on February 16, 1833, if less colorful than his reply to Hayne three years earlier, dwelt more fully and more cogently upon the constitutional issues at stake.

Against Calhoun's subtle and intricate logic Webster spoke as one dealing in plain matters of fact and common sense. He announced that he was going to tell what the Constitution actually was, not what it ought to be. It was not, as Calhoun argued, a compact between sovereign states who, in Calhoun's words, had *acceded* to it and conversely might *secede* from it. In its preamble the people of the United States had used no such language. "They do not say that they *accede* to a league, but they declare that they *ordain* and *establish* a Constitution." In their state ratifying conventions they agreed to adopt it. "They executed that agreement; they adopted the Constitution as a Constitution, and henceforth it must stand as a Constitution until it shall be altogether destroyed." It was an executed agreement to set up a government, a permanent one, supreme within its allotted sphere, acting directly on the nation as a whole. "The truth is, Mr. President, and no ingenuity of argument, no subtilty of distinction, can evade it, that, as to certain purposes, the people of the United States are one people. They are one in making war, and one in making peace; they are one in regulating commerce, and one in laying duties or imposts."

Having stated what the Constitution was, Webster disposed of secession as a revolutionary but not a constitutional right, then denounced nullification as no right at all. Its sponsors, he said, rejected "the first great principle of all republican liberty; that is, that the majority *must* govern." The alternatives were anarchy or despotism. "We hear loud and repeated denunciations against what is called *majority* government," he went on. "What, then, do gentlemen wish? Do they wish to establish a *minority* government? Do they wish to subject the will of the many to the will of the few?" The honorable gentleman from South Carolina had spoken of "absolute majorities and majorities concurrent," but that was language "wholly unknown to our Constitution," and language to which it was "not easy to affix definite ideas." Did not the honorable gentleman see how his argument against majorities might be turned upon him? Did the nullifiers practice what they preached? "Look to South Carolina, at the present moment. How far are the rights of minorities there respected?" Obviously the nullificationist majority was proceeding with a "relentless disregard" for the rights of the unionist minority — "a minority embracing, as the gentleman himself will admit, a large portion of the worth and respectability of the state."

Calhoun never answered that poser, never explained how minority rights in his own state were protected by nullification. He did come back at Webster, in ten days with a vigorous restatement of his "compact" theory. Afterward Calhoun and his friends were sure that he had won the argument, just as they had been with respect to Hayne three years before, and both times Webster and his admirers were equally confident that *he* had won.

In their appeals to the past Hayne and Calhoun and Webster all stood on rather dubious grounds. The nullifiers found in the Constitution occult meanings that Madison, one of its chief authors, could not discover. And Webster drew from its preamble — "we the people" — inferences that historically were not justified.

Calhoun and his followers could and did claim a victory in the immediate outcome of the nullification test. True, they failed to establish the constitutionality of the state veto or to prevent the passage of the bill for using Federal force against them. But they did defeat the administration's Verplanck bill and, co-operating with Clay, secured the adoption of his compromise tariff instead. At a reconvening of their state convention they rescinded their ordinance nullifying the previous tariffs, now superseded. Then, as if to have the last word, they nullified the recent force act, which would not have taken effect anyhow, since the original nullification ordinance had been withdrawn. They would not have had this face-saving opportunity if Webster had been able to carry Congress with him, for he held out to the last against any appeasement, any compromise.

Webster lost and yet he won. He was on the side of the winning future: in the years ahead his ideas and not Calhoun's were to prevail.

I V
Hate the Rich
1833–1836

> *"And whoever has the wickedness to conceive,
> and the hardihood to avow, a purpose to break
> down what has been found, in forty years' expe-
> rience, essential to the protection of all interests,
> by arraying one class against another, and by act-
> ing on such a principle as that the poor always hate
> the rich, shows himself the reckless enemy of all."*

THERE WERE GIANTS in the Senate in those days,
men of more than presidential stature, or so their admirers then and afterward believed.

There was Henry Clay, the tall Kentuckian with the
warm smile and the ready handshake, who looked like a
preacher but did not act like one. He was a hardy peren-
nial among presidential hopefuls. Already the voters had
turned him down twice, in 1824 and in 1832.

There was John C. Calhoun, the humorless "cast-iron
man" with a monomania on state rights. "He is wrought
like a piece of machinery, set going vehemently by a
weight, and stops while you answer," it seemed to Harriet
Martineau. "He either passes by what you say, or twists it

into suitability with what is in his head, and begins to lecture again." According to Jacksonians, he schemed to rule or ruin the Union, to make himself President of the whole or else of a seceded part.

And there was Daniel Webster, who more than any of his colleagues looked the part of the great man, with his magnificent head, his craggy brows, his deep-set luminous eyes. When at rest, he seemed a lion asleep. When he rose to speak — clothed in the colors of a Revolutionary soldier, in a buff vest and a dark blue coat with brass buttons — he began hesitantly, his right hand on his desk, his left hanging at his side. Once he was under way, his voice rose and fell in ringing, assured tones, while his left hand went behind his back, under his coattail, and his right got busy with vigorous gestures. His look and manner added conviction to his words. According to some who heard him, he spoke as "one under the true inspiration of seeing the invisible and grasping the impalpable," and with a single glance, "so expressive of intellectual power," he could refute whole volumes of an opponent's case.

Off stage, the incomparable actor could unbend in the company of his cronies, wealthy and highly civilized businessmen of Boston and New York. As the decanter passed back and forth he often became frolicsome as a schoolboy, full of funny stories, the "fiddle" of the party. "He talked like a book, and was pleasant as the morning twilight; his dark eyes looked like stars in their dark caverns," Philip Hone rhapsodized in his diary, after one cozy dinner of a few New York clubbists. On that occasion Webster displayed "none of those moody fits of abstraction which were wont to come over him at times."

To some of his comfortable and cultured intimates he seemed a veritable god, too much an Olympian for any earthly office, even the presidency, though they would have loved to see him in it. "The very thought (wild and hopeless as it is) of having Daniel Webster President of the United States," Hone wrote at election time in 1836, "should make the heart of every American leap in his bosom."

The wild and hopeless thought intrigued the senator himself. "Webster is ambitious, and can be satisfied with nothing short of the highest," his old New Hampshire acquaintance William Plumer thought in 1836. "He has acquired all the fame which mere speech-making can confer on him, but he has no substantial powers adequate to his desires or the acknowledged force of his mind." Plumer recalled a conversation one moonlit evening some years earlier as the two strolled about the Capitol grounds. All at once Webster "broke out into the most passionate aspirations after glory" and remarked ruefully that, at a younger age than he, Alexander the Great already had conquered the world.

Unfortunately for Webster, he was both too eager and too careless to be eligible for the highest honors in a democracy. As Miss Martineau observed, he seldom gave an impression of real sincerity. "His ambition for office, and for the good opinion of those who surround him, is seen too often in alternation with his love of ease and luxury to allow of his being confided in as he is admired." He had taken advantage of democratic institutions in order to rise in politics, but he was too unsympathetic with those institutions to rise still higher: he was at heart no democrat. "He is aristocratic in his tastes and habits, and but little republican simplicity is to be recognized in him."

That was a fatal handicap in the presidential politics of the 1830's, when a great many Americans looked upon elections as battles in a war of the classes, the poor against the rich.

2

As recently as 1820, Webster himself had warned against the day when the United States might become, through the influence of a protective tariff, a manufacturing nation with a large class of propertyless factory workers, a dangerous proletariat. Since then, the tariff with his blessing had been made a national policy and manufactures had prodigiously increased. Though profitable to some, the economic transformation of the North was painful to many, even in New England itself.

"With the exception of some Southerners, ruined by slavery," the well-traveled Miss Martineau reported, "I met no class in the United States so anxious about the means of living as the farmers of New England." On their poor and stony soil they had difficulty competing with farmers on the rich lands of the West, who sent their products cheaply to Eastern markets by way of the Great Lakes and the Erie Canal. Some of the Yankees went westward and took up new farms for themselves, and others migrated to the rising mill towns to look for factory work, but many remained on their unproductive acres, where they tried to make up their losses by borrowing, frequently from Boston insurance companies.

Among both farmers and artisans signs of class-consciousness appeared in a growing agitation against the Boston business group that dominated New England. Cries arose against the governing "aristocracy," the "commonwealth of property, of stocks, of machinery and of exclusive privileges," the "oligarchy of clubbists." A Workingmen's party entered local politics in 1833 and 1834, and though its members were mostly of the "middling class," they campaigned with slogans of hostility to the Boston "accumulators."

The Workingmen's movement was much more class-minded in New York. "In that city a separation is rapidly taking place between the different orders of society," wrote Thomas Hamilton, the British author of *Men and Manners in America* (1834). The "Workies" in New York were agitating for equal education as a means of doing away with the "aristocracy of knowledge." The more radical among them — the *"extrême gauche"* — also demanded an "agrarian law" for sharing the wealth through a periodic division of private property. As yet, said Hamilton, these agrarians were neither numerous nor widespread, but their party would multiply throughout the nation as population increased and wages fell. "Their ranks will always be recruited by the needy, the idle, and the profligate, and like a rolling snowball it will gather strength and volume, until at length it comes thundering with the force and desolation of an avalanche."

These fears Hamilton discussed with the men of affairs he met in the United States, among them Webster, and all agreed with him that the danger did exist, at least potentially. Some believed, however, that the crisis in this country would be averted by the benign influence of the frontier, by the accessibility of cheap government land,

which would draw off the population surplus from the
industrial centers of the East. Others "reckoned on education as a means of safety." Most of them assumed that
the revolutionary day was so far in the future that no one
need concern himself about it yet.

But Hamilton insisted that the day could not be postponed for long, not for more than, say, fifty years. "At
present the United States are perhaps more safe from revolutionary contention than any other country in the
world," he granted. "But this safety consists in one cir-
cumstance alone. *The great majority of the people are
possessed of property;* they have what is called a stake in
the hedge; and are therefore, by interest, opposed to all
measures which may tend to its insecurity. It is for such a
condition of society that the present constitution was
framed." When manufactures and population should have
increased to a certain point, however, the Constitution
would cease to fit the social facts. Then would come "the
great struggle between property and numbers."

The great struggle in this country seemed to develop
much sooner than even Thomas Hamilton had thought
it would. The great struggle was on, according to some
followers of Andrew Jackson, when they launched their
crusade against that monstrous "money power," the Bank
of the United States.

3

The Bank of the United States was a national bank. It
had been chartered by the Federal government, which
owned part of its stock, appointed some of its directors,

and kept deposits in it. From its headquarters in Philadelphia and its branches in other cities it performed indirectly some of the central banking functions of the later Federal Reserve System. Its president, the proud and poetic Nicholas Biddle, aimed to provide a businesslike administration and steer clear of politics. But the charter was due to expire in 1836, and to prolong the bank's life, Biddle was compelled to mix in politics, or so he gathered from his advisers, including Webster.

Webster was connected with the bank as legal counsel, director of the Boston branch, frequent borrower, and Biddle's friend. His advice Biddle sometimes took, as in appointing Webster's old friend Jeremiah Mason to head the Portsmouth branch, and sometimes rejected, as in refusing a heavy loan to the anti-Jackson *National Intelligencer* of Washington on the ground that it would be politically an unneutral act as well as financially a poor risk. When Jackson began to speak of the bank in distinctly hostile tones, Webster along with Clay and Biddle's Washington agent told Biddle he should apply to Congress for a recharter four years ahead of time, in 1832. If Jackson dared use his veto, Clay and Webster fondly thought, they would have an issue with which to defeat him in the presidential campaign.

In a Senate speech on the recharter bill Webster explained that his motives in supporting it were "not drawn from any local considerations." His own state, he said, did not need the bank as a source of capital, since she had plenty, nor "as any restraint or corrective on her own paper," since her banks were excellently conducted — as indeed they were, under the Suffolk System, through which they guaranteed one another's bank notes. But

Massachusetts was "interested that the general currency of the country should be maintained in a safe and healthy state," and she benefited along with others from the "facility of exchanges in internal commerce" which the bank afforded. This was "the sum of her motives" and, ostensibly, of Webster's.

Vetoing the bill, Jackson sent it back to Congress with a message in which he condemned the bank as unconstitutional, undemocratic, and un-American. Though Webster and Marshall long since had asserted its constitutionality in the case of *McCulloch* v. *Maryland*, Jackson insisted that the President had as much right and duty to interpret the Constitution as did the Supreme Court. The bank, he said, was a dangerous monopoly, which made the rich richer and the poor poorer, and which threatened to overpower the people's government itself. Many of the stockholders were foreigners who through the bank exercised a pernicious influence upon American affairs, he warned.

To Webster the veto was evil enough but the message was far worse. "It manifestly seeks to inflame the poor against the rich," he exclaimed in the Senate. "It wantonly attacks whole classes of the people, for the purpose of turning against them the prejudices and the resentments of other classes."

On the hustings he continued his horrified rebuttal. The investment of foreign funds in the bank, as in other American enterprises, he argued, was good for American business, good for the country, good for everyone except the "capitalist." "Every dollar brought from abroad, and put into the mass of active capital at home, by so much diminishes the rate of interest; and by so much, therefore, benefits all the active and trading classes of society, at the expense of the American capitalist." (By "capitalist," as he explained on a later occasion, he referred only to the rentier class.)

Webster's argument, however valid in itself, was not convincing to the majority of voters, and Clay as the candidate of the bank and of the National Republican party ran a very poor second to Jackson. The bank being now inextricably involved in politics, Biddle no longer hesitated to make loans to politicians and newspapermen who might be able to do the institution some good. He was preparing for a fight to the finish with the Jackson administration.

During the winter of 1832-1833, however, the nullification crisis intervened to distract attention from the bank and confuse the political scene. With Webster backing Jackson and force, and Clay backing Calhoun and compromise, Biddle's two great Senate champions drew apart, and a realignment of parties seemed at hand. Some of Webster's friends believed that Jackson's decisive stand against the nullifiers "would *necessarily* ultimately *lead to an alliance, offensive and defensive,* between Jackson and the Party that goes against the mis-called State Rights; for the judiciary, for internal improvements, for the tariff, and for the bank." From such a new alliance, according to rumor, Webster personally might have much to gain — a cabinet post soon, the presidency itself in time.

Biddle and his bank also might benefit from a rapprochement of Webster and Jackson, even though it should lead to an estrangement of Webster and Clay. Jackson was expected sooner or later to strike at the bank by withdrawing the government's deposits from it. As Jackson's ally, Webster could perhaps forestall the attack and possibly even get the charter renewed. Perhaps and possibly, but not for sure, and so Biddle dared not let relations between Clay and Webster deteriorate. "As for your friend Mr. W. (he is determined not to allow me to consider him mine)," Clay wrote to Biddle at the end of the congressional session in March 1833, "nothing I can do seems right in his mind." Clay asked Biddle to "soothe" Webster. "You hold a large flask of oil and know well how to pour it out." Biddle, while mediating between Webster and Clay, encouraged Webster to go ahead and cultivate the friendship of Jackson.

During the summer of 1833 the country was treated to a remarkable spectacle of billing and cooing between Jacksonians and Websterites. The President visited New England — where much to John Quincy Adams's disgust he received an honorary degree from Harvard — and was warmly greeted by Webster's political friends. The senator toured the West and was even more enthusiastically hailed by Jackson's followers. "Wherever he goes," the Louisville *Journal* reported, "the friends of the administration are peculiarly zealous to do him honor. The very men who, a year ago, were daily denouncing him as a Hartford convention traitor and the corrupt hireling of the Bank are now proud of the privilege of touching but the hem of his garment." The Pittsburgh *Advocate* compared his services to the Union with those of Jackson at New Orleans. He reciprocated by lauding the President — "true to his duty" in the eventful crisis of nullification — though confessing that he differed with him on internal improvements, the tariff, and the bank.

Not all the Jacksonians in the country welcomed the prospect of political bundling between Webster and Jackson. The hunchback Isaac Hill, a vitriolic New Hampshire editor and the dispenser of administration jobs in New England, preferred not to have to divide the spoils with new-found allies. Reminding his readers of Webster's Federalist and aristocratic proclivities, Hill played upon the prejudices of ordinary Yankees against the rich men of State Street. The new Vice President, Martin Van Buren, was even more determined than Hill to prevent a Webster-Jackson alliance. A soft-spoken master of the politician's art, Van Buren already had used his wiles to foster Jackson's quarrel with Calhoun and break up the Calhoun-Jackson combine. If he was to succeed to the presidency himself, he would have to keep Jackson and Webster apart. He maneuvered subtly to head off overtures between agents of the two men.

And Biddle himself lost interest in his scheme for cooperation between the two after the President, in September, finally got a Secretary of the Treasury who would carry out orders for removing the deposits. The new secretary, Roger B. Taney, ceased to put the government's money into the Bank of the United States and began to keep it in various state banks. The truce in the bank war was over. Biddle now turned to building up an anti-Jackson and pro-bank coalition for the next meeting of Congress.

But Webster hesitated about choosing sides, while he calculated his own interests in the controversy. If he went with Biddle's group he would have to clasp the hands of the nullifier Calhoun and the compromiser Clay, both of whom he lately had been exposing as enemies of the republic. He would have to condemn for executive usurpa-

tion against the bank the very President he had been ap-
plauding for his strong use of executive powers against
the State of South Carolina. And he would have to sub-
merge his presidential ambitions beneath those of Clay,
whose popular leadership of the National Republican
party long had been galling. If, on the other hand, he
stayed with Jackson he could continue to exploit the issue
of nationalism against nullification, with his full-throated
cry of the glorious Constitution, the glorious Union. And,
despite Van Buren's stratagems, he eventually might at-
tain the White House with Jackson's endorsement and
Jacksonian votes.

Whichever way he went, his presidential chances
seemed rather dubious and remote. There was for him
another consideration, more pressing, more immediate.
That, as usual, was money. At the end of 1833, after going to Washington for the Senate session, but before in-
dicating his decision to join the Biddle forces, Webster
sent the worried banker a little note: "Since I have arrived here, I have had an application to be concerned,
professionally, against the Bank, which I have declined,
of course, although I believe my retainer has not been
renewed, or *refreshed* as usual. If it be wished that my
relation to the Bank should be continued, it may be well
to send me the usual retainers."

4

Biddle had a scheme by which he intended to force the
administration to return the bank's deposits and renew
its charter. Singlehanded, he was going to bring on an

economic depression, which he could do by calling in loans and making credit scarce. The more people he could throw out of work, the better, so far as he was concerned. "Nothing but the evidence of suffering," he told the head of the Boston branch, would "produce any effect in Congress." He would excuse his action on the ground that the loss of the government deposits made it necessary.

Throughout the winter of 1833-1834 the Biddle panic was on. While businessmen found it difficult or impossible to borrow from the bank, politicians friendly to the institution got easy loans. These men stood to gain political as well as pecuniary benefits from the manufactured depression, since they could derive propaganda with which to discredit Jackson. All over the country they organized meetings to adopt petitions begging for relief from Congress, petitions which delegates then brought in person to Washington, and which pro-bank senators or representatives introduced with appropriately lugubrious speeches.

With such memorials Webster kept himself busy during the early months of 1834. His petitioners from Boston, he said, represented "American manual labor," were of "the muscular portion of society." Those from Philadelphia, three thousand in all, were carpenters, masons, brick-makers, bricklayers, painters and glaziers, lime-burners, plasterers, lumber merchants, and others who had to do with the building of houses. Those from Albany were unemployed wage-earners, and those from Ontario County, New York, were "farmers, mechanics, merchants, and other citizens." All together, from these and other places, Webster claimed to have indications of the sentiment of "nearly all practical men and men of business in the country, friends or foes of the administration."

From this mass of evidence Webster argued, convincingly enough, that economic distress was widespread and that workingmen were suffering the most. "American manual labor feels, or will feel, the shock more sensibly, far more sensibly, than capital or property of any kind," he declared. "Men in Albany, who three months ago were earning and receiving *a dollar and a quarter a day,* six days in the week, are now soliciting employment for two days in the week only, and for *sixty-two cents* a day." He further argued, with somewhat less conviction, that the administration was entirely to blame. The Jacksonians' contention that "all the excitement" had been "produced by the *bank,* by *panic-makers,* by *party politicians,*" he indignantly denied, although he knew it to be essentially the truth. "It is for those *who have changed the state of things,* it is for those *whose political acts have placed the country in the condition it now is in,* to take and bear the responsibility," he declaimed, and he meant the politicians on the Jackson side.

During these harangues the imperturbable Van Buren, in the presiding officer's chair, listened with an innocent and attentive manner, as if he treasured every word to repeat it faithfully to the President. After Clay eloquently had seconded one of Webster's motions to have a memorial printed, Van Buren left his chair, went up to Clay, asked for a pinch of his snuff, then nonchalantly walked off. But Van Buren was neither so innocent nor so impartial as he pretended to be. In fact, he was preparing a rabble-rousing speech against the bank to be delivered by a member of his New York State political machine, one of the sturdiest Jacksonians on the Senate floor, Silas Wright.

Wright, at the time of his election in 1833, was the youngest of the senators, only thirty-seven. He was not much to look at — short and stocky, with the red nose and red face of a heavy drinker — but he was a plain and forceful speaker, more effective than one would gather from Webster's contemptuous comment that in debate he always skipped the "hard places." Earlier, as a member of the House committee that framed the tariff bill of 1828, Wright had given Webster considerable trouble. Now, with Van Buren's script, which assailed the bank and its allies as enemies of the common people, he again presented a challenge to Webster.

Webster replied in tones of anguish and anger. "It has been proclaimed that one thing was certain, that there was always a hatred on the part of the poor toward the rich, and that this hatred would support the late measures, and the putting down of the bank," he began. "Sir, the very man, of all others, who has the deepest interest in a sound currency, and who suffers most by mischievous legislation in money matters, is the man who earns his daily bread by his daily toil." The Jacksonians, in raising the cry of class struggle, were Catalines "greedy of other men's property and prodigal of their own." They, and not the bank men, were the real enemies of the common people. Anyone who talked like Wright was a public enemy. "An enemy to his whole country, to all classes, and to every man in it, he deserves to be marked especially as *the poor man's curse!*"

This tirade, for all its thunderous indignation, did not inspire so much applause as might have been expected among the bankers and other businessmen along Boston's State Street. Some of them had begun to suspect that Biddle, more than Wright or Jackson himself, was at the moment the curse of the country. They appointed a committee to present their case to Congress, naming Nathan Appleton as a member precisely because he "was of opinion that Mr. Biddle had already carried the system of contraction farther than was necessary." On the way to Washington the Boston committee conferred with a similar New York group. In New York they "found the dissatisfaction with Mr. Biddle very ripe," as Appleton afterward reported. The New Yorkers had given Biddle "an ultimatum, which he must accept, or be denounced at the adjourned public meeting as unnecessarily pressing upon the mercantile community." While in New York, Appleton and his associates chanced to meet Biddle, and they took the opportunity to tell him "some home truths" — that their community "ought not and would not sustain him in further pressure, which he very well knew was not necessary for the safety of the bank, and in which his whole object was to coerce a charter." Biddle listened, but they "could get very little from him but the merest commonplace."

Webster, caught between his client and his constituents, sent word to Biddle that he ought to contract his loans as slowly and as moderately as he could, occasionally letting up in order to relieve hardships and offset the rising clamor against the bank. And Biddle, to appease the New York and Boston businessmen, did lighten his pressure on the money markets, but only for a month. After that, he renewed it more violently than ever. Then, when Congress had adjourned, he reversed himself again and rapidly increased the bank's discounts. The Biddle panic was over.

It had failed to help the bank. During the session Webster had sponsored a recharter bill with modifications intended to disarm the opposition. The new charter was to run for only six years, to grant no exclusive rights, and to prohibit the issue of bank notes in denominations of less than twenty dollars. This compromise proposal, with its concessions to the foes of monopoly and of paper money, came presumably from Biddle himself. In pressing it, however, Webster had to contend against the competing plans of Clay, who insisted on a charter to last the full twenty years, and Calhoun, who talked of "unbanking the banks" somehow with one to run for twelve. If the bank men had got together, they could have put a recharter bill through the Senate, though not the House.

One thing they did accomplish, but it was only a gesture of partisan vindictiveness. This was a Senate resolution solemnly censuring the President for his removal of the deposits. Webster, more interested in benefiting Biddle than in condemning Jackson, had concentrated his attention on the recharter bill rather than the resolution of censure, though in the end he voted for it. When Jackson responded with an official protest, Webster defended the action of the Senate but confessed that he personally was sorry about the conflict with the President. "The present occasion of difference has not been sought or made by me," he avowed. "It is thrust upon me, in opposition to strong opinions and wishes, on my part not concealed."

Had it been otherwise, had he been able to stay on friendly terms with both Biddle and Jackson, his chances for the presidency at the next election very likely would have been much better than they actually were.

5

The bank issue having intervened, Webster could not capitalize upon the nullification crisis to found a new party on a simple Constitution and Union platform. The memory of his famous replies to Hayne and Calhoun did get him a presidential nomination, but only from a group of his devotees in the Massachusetts legislature, who at the beginning of 1835 raised his nationalist standard and named him as its bearer for the campaign of 1836. And party lines were being redrawn, but not in a way that favored his candidacy.

Jackson's followers, previously known as Democratic Republicans, now called themselves plain Democrats. His opponents, formerly the National Republicans, adopted the name of Whigs. Thereby they implied that the Jacksonians were Tories, upholders of the tyrannical pretensions of "King Andrew I," whose heir presumptive was Van Buren. Though the anti-Jacksonians had a name, they had not a party, not a coherent national organization. They were a congeries of factions with little in common save their unanimous antagonism to Jackson and Van Buren.

The task for Webster, as for any other Whig aspirant, was to attract to his support as many as possible of these discordant groups. And he began early to woo one of them, the Antimasons, who in a few states had made a going political concern out of denunciations of the secret and exclusive, and hence presumably undemocratic and un-American, Freemasonic Lodge. He assured the Massachusetts Antimasons that he and his father before him had always disliked the society. That, if true, should have been hard to explain, since he and his father had admired without qualification that thirty-third degree Mason, George Washington. More relevant, no doubt, was the fact that Webster's contemporaries Jackson and Clay were also Masons. But the Antimasons of Massachusetts did not respond very enthusiastically to Webster's overtures. Neither did those of Pennsylvania. When a national Antimasonic convention met in Harrisburg, Webster was not even second choice for President.

The first choice of the Antimasons, and of the Whigs in Pennsylvania and the West, was the Indian-fighting hero of Tippecanoe and the War of 1812, General William Henry Harrison. Webster could not compete with Harrison in popularity, most Whig politicians believed. His past was against him. "Ah, but he was a Federalist! Damning sin! Never to be forgiven! But he was opposed to the war!" So the politicians said, as a Pennsylvania correspondent reported to Webster. An Ohio correspondent warned him that the Whig party "deceived itself by consulting and taking counsel almost exclusively from those in the highest walks of life. The rank and file of men, however, poll the votes." And Webster, according to reputation, had little concern for the rank and file. Indeed, he was quoted in Democratic newspapers as having said: "Let Congress take care of the Rich, and the Rich will take care of the Poor." When his distant cousin Noah Webster appealed to him, he disavowed this statement, but he was on the defensive.

Most of the Whig newspapers backed Webster until his prospects became entirely hopeless, and his campaign managers in Boston stayed with him even after his chances had disappeared. These men, who included such merchants and manufacturers as Abbott Lawrence, strove almost to the last to unite the Whig party behind the favorite son of Massachusetts. They sent out circular letters to editors and politicians throughout the country. Webster himself wrote repeatedly to Biddle, begging him to use his great influence for the Whig cause, which Webster obviously identified with his own.

Biddle, however, was no single-minded Webster partisan. His strategy was to run three Whig candidates, each supposedly strong in one section of the country: Webster in New England, Harrison in Pennsylvania and the West, Hugh Lawson White of Tennessee in the South. "This disease is to be treated as a local disorder — apply local remedies — if General Harrison will run better than anybody else in Pennsylvania, by all means unite upon him." Such was Biddle's diagnosis and prescription. None of the three candidates could expect to get a majority in the electoral college, but separately they might possibly prevent Van Buren from getting a majority. The election then would devolve, as in 1824-1825, upon the House of Representatives, where conceivably the Whigs might be able to elect one of their men.

The more realistic Whig leaders privately confessed defeat long before Election Day. As early as the spring of 1835 William H. Seward explained to his partner, the Whig boss of New York, Thurlow Weed, why Van Buren was bound to win. "The people are for him. Not so much for him as for the principle they suppose he represents. That principle is Democracy," Seward wrote to Weed. "It is with them the poor against the rich, and it is not to be disguised that, since the last election, the array of parties has very strongly taken that character. Those who felt themselves or believed themselves poor have fallen off very naturally from us, and into the majority . . . while 'the rich *we* have always with us.' " The Whig papers, Seward added, had maneuvered themselves unconsciously into the politically indefensible position of apologizing for the rich.

Webster himself, as Election Day approached, became as pessimistic as Seward but rationalized his forthcoming defeat in more personal terms. In September 1836 William Plumer found that Webster "felt sore at his own ill success in the canvass" and "imputed some part of his apparent unpopularity to Clay." Having failed to put himself at the head of Jackson's opponents, Webster was envious of his more popular Whig rival. "He feels that Clay, though his inferior in many respects, is yet the acknowledged leader of the Whig party."

The returns that fall confirmed the worst fears of Webster. He carried the State of Massachusetts, with forty-two thousand votes to Van Buren's thirty-four thousand, but that was all.

V
The New Democracy
1836–1840

"If they mean the new democracy — the cry against credit, against industry, against labor, against a man's right to leave his own earnings to his own children — why, then, doubtless they are right; all this sort of democracy is theirs. But if by democracy they mean a conscientious and stern adherence to the true popular principles of the Constitution and the government, then I think they have very little claim to it."

He is fifty-seven years old, and looks worn and furrowed," Chancellor James Kent of New York wrote in his diary after dining with Daniel Webster in the summer of 1840. "His belly becomes protuberant, and his eyes deep in his head." He drank too much.

His personal finances had become more complicated than ever. The nation was slowly recovering, but he was never to recover, from the panic of '37.

From 1835 to 1837 he along with many of his fellow Americans had reveled in a boom. Money was easy, especially after the state banks were freed from the controlling hand of the Bank of the United States, and the bank itself, continuing in business with a Pennsylvania charter, joined in the wildcat practices of the others. Speculators borrowed bank notes and used them to pay for tracts of government land in the West. The government did a veritable land-office business, though it was giving up good real estate for paper of uncertain value. English capital poured into the country to be invested in corporation stocks and state bonds as well as Federal lands. Many of the states went deeply into debt to finance the construction of roads and canals and railways, and so did private companies, digging ditches and laying tracks here, there, and everywhere.

No one was more virulently infected than Webster with the speculative fever of the time, and no one did more to stimulate it. In the Senate he helped to carry through Clay's plan for distributing among the various states the surplus revenue of the Federal government, which for the only years of its history was out of debt, thanks to land sales. He justified the distribution bill as an inflationary measure which would "remove the severe and almost unparalleled pressure for money" and make possible continuing investment in private business and public land. Meanwhile, through agents on the spot, he avidly bought prairies and timberland and townsites in Ohio, Michigan, Wisconsin, and Illinois. Rising prices seemed to guarantee him a fortune in a few years.

There were signs of trouble ahead, for those who cared to see them. The cost of living, as usual, rose faster than wages, and the purchasing power of laborers declined. That of many farmers did the same when they suffered a succession of crop failures. Sources of foreign funds dried up as banks in England began to close their doors. But

Webster like others kept converting bank notes into real estate. Finally the Federal government called a halt, when Jackson's Specie Circular forbade the sale of public land except for hard money or the notes of specie-paying banks. Soon afterward, in early 1837, came the crash.

It left Webster land-poor, with some twelve thousand acres on his hands. In the summer of 1837 he visited the West and looked over his holdings, finding many of them magnificent enough but few of them salable for the time being. In the summer of 1839 he took a trip to England and, while there, tried to peddle some of his properties.

His venture in Western lands aggravated his already incorrigible borrowing habits. Most of his acquaintances he sooner or later honored with a request for a loan, which eventually turned into a gift. So Caleb Cushing learned after Webster asked him for three thousand dollars to pay a land agent who demanded cash to complete a transaction when the Specie Circular ruled out the usual bank notes. Instead of paying Cushing back, Webster repeatedly asked for more as the years went by. At the time of his death the debt amounted to ten thousand, which Cushing never was able to collect. And Cushing was only one of a number of thwarted creditors.

These unpaid loans did not suffice for Webster's pecuniary appetite. Nor did his legal fees, though they sometimes amounted to as much as twenty-five thousand dollars. Besides these sources of income and his Senate salary, he was beginning to need outright subsidies from the constituents he served. While he hinted that he might have to leave the Senate and devote himself to his law practice, his friend Edward Everett appealed to Thomas W. Ward, treasurer of Harvard College and American agent for the English bankers Baring Brothers, to canvass the Boston businessmen for a trust fund of a hundred thousand dollars to keep him in public life. The party battle, Everett said, was "nothing less than a war of Numbers against Property," and Webster was indispensable to "our friends in Boston" for the protection of "their houses, their lands, their stocks."

The coming of hard times heightened social tensions. By threatening his wealthy constituents with revolution, it increased their dependence upon Webster while, by threatening him with bankruptcy, it increased his dependence upon his wealthy constituents.

2

In the Senate the leaders of the opposition — Webster, Clay, Calhoun — were acting in unison as Jackson's second term drew to a close. They were fighting as a team, though futilely, against the effort of Democrats to clear the name of the outgoing President. The Democrats were determined to "expunge" from the Senate record the three-year-old resolution censuring Jackson for his removal of the government's deposits from the Bank of the United States.

The chief expunger was Thomas Hart Benton, once Jackson's foe in a wild frontier brawl, now one of his most dependable allies. This backwoods intellectual from Missouri never hesitated to display his homespun erudition. To many of his enemies, as to Harriet Martineau, he seemed a "mock heroic Senator" as at his desk he "sat swelling amid his piles of books and papers." To Webster's crony Philip Hone he was the "fiercest tiger in the den," yet he and Webster respected one another and remained personally on good terms. He hated Calhoun. When a duel between the two was rumored, Hone commented that Calhoun could no more properly accept a challenge from Benton than one — to change the zoological metaphor — from a hyena.

In his memoirs Benton, as literate as any of his detractors, left a dramatic and detailed account of the final expunging, to him a most historic event. The Senate chamber was jammed, the great chandelier was lit, and the expungers — with "an ample supply of cold hams, turkeys, rounds of beef, pickles, wines and cups of hot coffee" — were ready for an all-night session. Calhoun, then Clay, then Webster spoke at agonizing length as the Whigs attempted to filibuster. Near midnight they gave up, and Benton had the immense satisfaction of seeing the secretary of the Senate open the original manuscript journal, draw a square of broad black lines around the sentence condemning Jackson, and write across it in a bold hand the words: "Expunged by order of the Senate, this 16th day of January, 1837."

As Whigs saw it, this desecration of the Senate's inviolable books was but another crime of executive despotism. But Whigs could hope that it was the last. With Jackson out and Van Buren in, they could expect to hold their own against the administration and even to recover some lost ground. For Van Buren would not be the man that Jackson had been, and the economic depression, now real, could be used more cogently than Biddle's artificial panic as an argument against the party in power.

On the way home after Van Buren's inauguration Webster laid down the lines of the opposition's new campaign when, at the invitation of his merchant friends, who had arranged a mass demonstration to dissuade him from resigning his Senate seat, he addressed a yelling, window-breaking throng in the great hall of Niblo's Saloon in New York. His speech was a masterpiece of partisan indictment, his manner dignified, his attitude seemingly objective. Picturing the country as on the way to ruin, he explained the nation's troubles as the inevitable consequence of economic stupidity, of Jackson's policies in regard to money and banking. He called upon the American people to combine against a continuation of these disastrous blunders under Jackson's successor. If the cheers in Niblo's Saloon could be taken as an index of public opinion, Webster for the moment had the people on his side.

But the new President had no intention of retreating. He planned to go ahead with the Jacksonian idea of a "divorce" between the government and the banks. The government would confine itself to cash transactions, receiving and paying out only specie, and keeping its money in subtreasuries in various cities. This scheme did not please all the enemies of the old Bank of the United States. The advocates of easy money had objected to the bank because it checked the propensities of the state banks to manufacture bank notes; the subtreasury scheme would be more restrictive still. On the other hand, the plan pleased the advocates of hard money, who had objected to the bank because they wanted coin as currency and no bank notes at all. The Senate champion of the hard-money men was Benton — "Old Bullion."

When the Senate met again, for its first session of the Van Buren administration, Benton acquired an unexpected ally and Webster an unexpected foe. Calhoun was now on the administration's side, ready to support the subtreasury bill.

Another issue, however, complicated the realignment of senators, the issue of slavery and the slave trade. Antislavery societies throughout the North were flooding Congress with petitions to end the interstate traffic in human chattels and abolish slavery itself in the District of Columbia. On these matters Benton was inclined to agree with Webster, and Clay with Calhoun.

Taking the orthodox position of most Democrats and Whigs alike — "this government has, constitutionally, nothing to do with slavery, as it exists in the states" — Webster would have been glad to let the whole subject go at that. But Calhoun kept forcing the issue. He insisted that the Senate should agree to reject automatically all petitions regarding slavery, as the House had done. He introduced a resolution which declared that the "intermeddling" of citizens of any state to abolish slavery in the District of Columbia would amount to a "dangerous attack" on the people of the slaveholding states. Coming to his support, Clay added a resolution that any act of Congress looking toward abolition in the District would be a "violation of the faith" implied in the cessions of land for the national capital by the slaveholding states of Virginia and Maryland.

Webster had to take a stand against Calhoun and Clay if he was to keep the respect of his constituents, who sent him petition after antislavery petition, one of them signed by four hundred and thirty-three citizens of Boston.

"Among these signers," he said, in proposing their memorial to the Senate, "I recognize the names of many persons well known to me as gentlemen of great worth and respectability. They are clergymen, lawyers, merchants, literary men, manufacturers, and indeed persons from all classes of society." He firmly expressed his "honest opinion" that Congress did have the constitutional power to deal with slavery and the slave trade in the District and should receive and consider petitions on the subject.

But he tried again and again to shift the discussion to other grounds entirely. The real question, he maintained, was presidential despotism — the "design to extend executive authority, not only in derogation of the just powers of Congress, but to the danger of the public liberty." He reminded Calhoun that lately they had been co-operating against the tyranny of Andrew Jackson. Suppose Jackson now should walk into the Senate chamber "and see into whose hands has fallen the chief support of that administration which was, in so great a degree, appointed by himself and which he fondly relied on to maintain the principles of his own"! Webster pled with Calhoun to "come back now" and "exert his acknowledged ability" to put an end to the "mischiefs of reckless experiments and dangerous innovation," the most reckless and dangerous of which was the overthrow of the Bank of the United States and the proposed substitution for it of the subtreasury system.

Lacking Calhoun's support, Webster was able during the Van Buren administration to achieve only one small and temporary success for his monetary views. His resolution to repeal the Specie Circular passed both the Senate and the House. "Verily, Wall Street rejoiceth!" Hone exulted in his diary. "Stocks have risen and domestic exchanges have fallen, and it would seem that the touch of Webster (as he said on a certain occasion of that of Alexander Hamilton) has caused the corpse of public credit to rise on its feet and stand erect." But the administration failed to carry out the intent of Congress, and Hone soon noted sadly that a "blight" had come upon "our bright prospects."

Against the subtreasury scheme itself, Webster could fight only a rearguard action. The bill twice passed the Senate, only to fail in the House, then finally (in 1840) was carried through both. The government and the banks were divorced. Benton again was triumphant.

3

Conflicting views of American society, already evoked by Jackson's war with the bank, were elaborated during the discussion of Van Buren's subtreasury plan, as the onset of depression gave a heightened sense of urgency to the debate. To the question of social realities and possibilities in the United States, there were at least three approaches: radical, reactionary, and conservative. The most prominent though not the most profound exponent of the radicalism of the time was Van Buren, and the foremost advocate of reaction Calhoun. Their rapprochement marked a general combination of radicals and reactionaries within the Democratic party. Against this meeting of extremes, Webster defended a conservative middle ground.

Originating with the Locofocos, the left-wing Democrats of the Northeast, and gaining currency in the writings of various Jacksonian intellectuals, the radical philosophy found authoritative expression in Jackson's message vetoing the bank bill and in the antibank speech that Van Buren wrote for Silas Wright. The radicals assumed the existence of gross inequalities and serious social conflict but, while they talked of revolutionary dangers, they did not generally advocate revolutionary violence. Instead, they proposed the elimination of government favors to private enterprise, the destruction of government-granted monopolies and other corporate privileges, which supposedly were to blame for economic inequality and popular distress. The radical impetus came from artisans, shopkeepers, and small businessmen who assumed that, if freed from governmental interference, they would prosper in just proportion to their own individual efforts.

Now, Calhoun had no concern for either the wage-earners or the petty capitalists of the North, except as prospective voters. The very embodiment of the slavery interest, he centered his thoughts upon the welfare of the slaveholders of the South, though as an aspirant for the presidency he was willing to make concessions to his own ambition. What he really wanted was an alliance of Southern planters and Northern capitalists such as might, on the one hand, guarantee the slave economy and, on the other, make him President.

He based much of his political and social thinking on a concept of the class struggle. The contemporary Locofocos endorsed this concept, but Calhoun developed it further and found in it implications more startling. Long before Marx, he predicted that capitalist society would tend to

divide into only two classes, "capitalists" and "operatives," that the former would expropriate and impoverish
the latter, and that a revolutionary crisis would eventuate.
The crisis itself, he hoped and expected, would throw
the capitalists into the arms of the planters, whose aid
they would seek against the class enemy of both. He kept
awaiting the critical day, and during the Biddle panic he
thought it was at hand: soon the capitalists would come
around. "They begin to feel," he congratulated himself,
"that they have more to fear from their own people than
we have from our slaves." Though the panic disappointed
him he continued to be confident that, as industry grew,
the "tendency to conflict in the North" would increase.
In 1837 he announced frankly to his fellow senators:
"There is and always has been in an advanced stage of
wealth and civilization a conflict between labor and capital."

Here Calhoun was taking his stand with the Democrats
and against the Whigs, but he had made the switch from
Clay and Webster to Benton and Van Buren not so much
because of principle as because of expediency. He was
himself no social revolutionary: his object in proclaiming
the development of class conflict was to postpone or to
prevent and not to hasten the outbreak of mass revolt.
But the representatives of Northern business, such as
Webster, had shown little or no inclination to approve
the kind of planter-capitalist alliance that Calhoun en-
visaged. The businessmen were not ready to join the
planters on his terms, which included his system of state
rights and nullification. And their party, the Whigs,
seemed to offer little either for his personal advancement
or for the protection of his favorite institution. In the

North the Whigs were infected with the antislavery virus, and they were "consolidationists," proponents of a consolidated government with powers to carry out banking, tariff, and improvements policies in disregard of planter interests and state rights. True, the Democrats also acted like consolidationists at times, as in the case of Jackson's stand on nullification, but they seemed more immune to abolitionism than the Whigs, more sound on Federal powers and policies, and more likely to accept him as a presidential nominee.

As the extremes of right and left came together against the middle, Democrats denounced banks and other corporations and defended slavery not only in the national forum at Washington but also within the states, as at the Pennsylvania constitutional convention of 1837-1838. There the Locofoco delegates contended that all corporations were "unrepublican and radically wrong," that "labor performed for corporations" was "like the labor of slaves," and that, if Northern abolitionists were allowed to go South and stir up slaves against masters, then Southern agitators would be justified in going North and arousing workers against employers. Thaddeus Stevens, spokesman for property in the Pennsylvania convention as Webster and Kent had been years earlier in the Massachusetts and New York conventions, expressed his horror at this suggestion and referred sarcastically to the "appropriate alliance" being formed "between the radical reformers of the North and the lawless nullifiers of the South." Then and afterward Stevens tried to break up this alliance and win the common man to the support of business interests by preaching a gospel of antislavery "democracy" against the "aristocracy" of slaveholders.

A more authentic voice of big business, Webster in the Senate played down the question of slavery. He made his central theme the potential harmony of all interests and all classes. What was good for the businessmen of Boston and Philadelphia and New York, he assumed, was good for everybody, rich and poor, North and South.

"In the old countries of Europe there is a clear and well-defined line between capital and labor," he conceded to Calhoun and the radicals, but he denied that there was a line so "broad, marked, and visible" in the United States. Who in this country were laborers, and who capitalists? Why, he said, practically all Americans (he meant Northerners) belonged to "the working classes" or "the industrious classes," with which he lumped "the active men of business." The "capitalists," as he used that term, included only those who lived exclusively on income from property. "If this property be land, they live on rent; if it be money, they live on its interest."

The distinction between American classes, already vague and indistinct, was on the way to becoming non-existent, thanks to the workings of a beneficent economy. "This distinction grows less and less definite as commerce advances," Webster declared, contradicting Calhoun; "the effect of commerce and manufactures, as all history shows, being everywhere to diffuse wealth and not to aid its accumulation in few hands." Look at Massachusetts! "I do not believe there is on earth, in a highly civilized society, a greater equality in the condition of men than exists there. If there be a man in the state who maintains what is called an equipage, has servants in livery, or drives four horses in his coach, I am not acquainted with him," Webster exclaimed. And he added that the "condition of the

great mass of the people" was constantly improving because of business enterprise and the progress of technology, the introduction of labor-saving or rather "labor-
doing" machines.

If there was any revolutionary discontent among the
American people, Webster thundered, it was due chiefly
to the clamor of irresponsible and self-interested agitators. "In a country of perfect equality, they would move
heaven and earth against privilege and monopoly. In a
country where property is more equally divided than anywhere else, they rend the air with the shouting of agrarian doctrines. In a country where the wages of labor are
high beyond all parallel, and where lands are cheap, and
the means of living low, they would teach the laborer
that he is but an oppressed slave. Sir, what can such men
want? What do they mean? They can want nothing, Sir,
but to enjoy the fruits of other men's labor."

If at the moment the people were suffering, as many of
them were, from bankruptcies and unemployment, that
was due to the fiscal policies of the agrarians themselves.
"The prosperity of the working classes," Webster said,
"lives, moves, and has its being in established credit and
a steady medium of payment." But the Jacksonians had
destroyed the going system of money and credit. "Who
are they that profit by the present state of things? They
are not the many, but the few." In this deflationary time
of high interest rates the "speculators" and "dealers in
money" did very well, but the "small capitalists" and "all
classes of labor" were up against calamity. So, according
to Webster, the self-proclaimed friends of the common
man were in truth his worst enemies.

The great harmonizer of all interests, as Webster now

saw it, was a wise and active Federal government stimulating and regulating economic activity by means of a national banking system, a protective tariff, and expenditures for internal improvements.

Most important was the banking system. "Every bank, as banks are now constituted in this country, performs two distinct offices or functions," he explained to the merchants of New York. First, every bank discounted bills or notes; that is, it made loans. Second, in making loans it issued "paper with an express view to circulation," its own bank notes, which became a part of the "circulating medium," the nation's money. With "each individual bank acting from the promptings of its own interest" and "not from any sense of public duty," the amount of money "afloat at any time in the community" might swell to a dangerously inflationary extent. "Hence arises my view of the duty of government to take the care and control of the issues of these local institutions," said Webster. "What we need, and what we must have, is some currency which shall be equally acceptable in the Gulf of Mexico, in the valley of the Mississippi, on the Canada frontier, on the Atlantic Ocean, and in every town, village, and hamlet of our extended land." Only a national bank could provide that.

The conservative philosophy of Webster thus had no place for *laissez faire*. When Silas Wright proposed that the government tend to its own business and let the people attend to theirs, Webster expressed his horror at this "ominous" and "ill-boding" doctrine which constituted "the whole principle and policy of the administration, at the present critical moment." And when Calhoun objected that credit was private property, and that the government had no right to interfere with it, Webster replied: "Government does interfere and place restrictions in a thousand ways upon every kind of individual property; and it is done, and is necessarily done, by every government, for the good of the whole community."

Not just bankers and businessmen stood to gain by such governmental interference, and not just bankers and businessmen stood to lose by the "divorce" of government and banks. The subtreasury system would benefit no one (except the "capitalists" in the Websterian sense). "It withdraws specie from the circulation and from the banks, and piles it up in useless heaps in the treasury." But the "credit system" raised the "great mass of men" to a high standard of living. It benefited the planters of the South, who needed credit and sound money in the growing and marketing of their cotton crop. It connected "labor and capital, by giving to labor the use of capital." Take away this credit, and what was left? "If we curtail the general business of society, does not every laboring man find his condition grow daily worse?" What helps business helps everybody.

As for internal improvements, they helped the whole country, not merely the localities in which they lay. "Whatsoever promotes communication, whatsoever extends general business, whatsoever encourages enterprise, or whatsoever advances the general wealth and prosperity of other states," as Webster told the citizens of Bangor, Maine, in the northeastern corner of the country, "must have a plain, direct, and powerful bearing on your own prosperity."

And the tariff, he assured Calhoun, did not fall unequally upon the South: Northerners as well as Southerners paid duties on imported articles; Southerners as well as Northerners profited by the development of a home market for their products. "For myself," declared Webster, "I fully and conscientiously believe that, in regard to this whole question, the interest of the North and East is entirely reconcilable to the real, solid, and permanent interest of the South and West."

He professed to be baffled by Calhoun's desertion to Van Buren. "A principal object in his late political movements, the gentleman himself tells us, was to *unite the entire South;* and against whom, or against what, does he wish to unite the entire South?" Webster asked. "He now tells us . . . that he marches off under the states-rights banner! Let him go. I remain. I am where I have ever been, and ever mean to be. Here, standing on a platform broad enough and firm enough to uphold every interest of the whole country."

Of course, Webster in fact was not quite where he had always been. Once he had stood for state rights and *laissez faire,* had warned against industrialism and the rise of a working class. He did remain consistent in holding to one fundamental tenet of his earlier philosophy, though no longer emphasizing it. This was his belief that property and power went and should go together. As he told a Pittsburgh audience (in 1833): "To be free, the people must be intelligently free; to be substantially independent, they must be able to secure themselves against want, by sobriety and industry; to be safe depositories of political power, they must be able to comprehend and understand the general interests of the community, and must themselves have a stake in the welfare of that community."

But, throughout the 1830's, Webster contended that only Whig policies — the bank, the tariff, internal improvements — would diffuse prosperity and property among the people, maintain and extend their stake in society, and re-establish the harmony of interests which, he charged, Jacksonian misgovernment had upset.

4

While Webster was losing the legislative battle in the Senate, he was also losing important cases in the Supreme Court. He no longer had a friend as chief justice after the death of John Marshall in 1835. Marshall's successor, Roger B. Taney, was a Jacksonian of Jacksonians, the very man who as Secretary of the Treasury had carried out Jackson's order to remove the government deposits from the Bank of the United States. Once at the head of the Court, Taney with a majority of his associates began to modify some of the principles that Marshall and Webster had established in defense of corporations.

In the Charles River Bridge case (1837) Taney held, against the argument of Webster, that the Commonwealth of Massachusetts, when it chartered the original toll-bridge company, had not estopped itself forever after from authorizing a competitive free bridge. According to Jacksonian doctrine, now sanctified by the Court, corporation charters should be construed in favor of the public interest, even if at the expense of vested rights. This differed from the view that Webster had advanced and Marshall had upheld in the Dartmouth College case.

In the case of the Bank of Augusta, Georgia (1838), Taney faced the question whether corporations chartered in one state could make contracts enforceable in another state. Webster, attorney for the bank, contended that a corporation had the same rights as a person, and he quoted the clause of the Constitution that guaranteed citizens of one state the privileges and immunities of citizens of any other. Ruling against him, Taney postponed until after the Civil War judicial acceptance of the idea that a corporation was a person.

That the Court was the final arbiter of constitutional questions, Webster could not well deny, since he had done as much as anyone to secure both judicial and popular acceptance of that view. The only recourse, for him and others who disliked the new judicial line, was to get control of the presidency and thereby, ultimately, the Court.

5

As they looked forward to the campaign of 1840, Whig politicians could not be sure of winning with a candidate so closely identified with unpopular causes as Webster was. Long before nomination time the Whig papers one by one dropped him. Clay, on the other hand, thought he himself would be a certain winner. Through a mutual friend in Boston he tried to persuade Webster to withdraw and give him another chance. Reluctantly Webster made up his mind to step aside, but not for Clay. While in England he announced his decision not to run. After his return the Webster men went for William Henry Harrison and helped to nominate him. "Now that we have got the *Clay*

off our wheels," Webster heard from his son-in-law Samuel
Appleton, "we shall get along."

The Whig vehicle did not have any Clay (or any Webster) to hold it back; neither did it have any baggage, any
statement of party aims, to weight it down. In the previous
presidential campaign the Whigs had been unable to get
going because, as Seward then told Weed, they were
looked upon as partisans of the wealthy. Now — with Seward, Weed, and their journalistic partner Horace Greeley
directing the campaign — the Whigs set out to prove as little as possible except that Van Buren was an aristocrat and
Harrison a common man.

With the hero of Tippecanoe at the head of their ticket,
they stole the military glamor of the Jackson party, and
with John Tyler in second place they gave credibility to
their claim to being the real Democratic party, since Tyler
was a Virginia Democrat. They received a propaganda gift
when the editor of a Van Buren paper made a sneering
reference to Harrison as a man who, but for the Whig politicians, would have been content to spend his life guzzling
hard cider in a backwoods cabin. They seized upon the log
cabin and the cider jug as symbols of their democracy, and
the jug was not so empty as their slogan: "Tippecanoe and
Tyler too!"

The time had not yet arrived when a presidential candidate might, with propriety, stump for himself, but Harrison had no need to, as the party covered the country with
able campaigners, including the two most famous political
orators of the period, Webster and Clay. Both of them,
their own ambitions thwarted, might have had excuse for
sulking in their separate tents, but neither did so. Despite
his worn and furrowed look, his protuberant belly and his

sunken eyes, Webster toured like a gallant trouper for the grand Whig show. His circuit took him through the states of the Northeast and as far south as Virginia.

Early in the campaign, on August 19, 1840, at Saratoga, New York, he put on his greatest performance of the season and one of the greatest in the history of American electioneering. At Saratoga, a few minutes after he had begun to speak in a hilltop pine grove, the jerry-built speaker's platform collapsed, and he and the local Whig dignitaries with him fell eight feet to the ground. Amid the scramble he was the first to get to his feet. With unruffled dignity he assured the audience that no one was hurt and that the "great Whig platform" was far more solid than the structure he had just been standing on. Then he mounted a farm wagon covered with planks and from that improvised rostrum resumed his address. He kept it up for nearly three hours.

The theme of his speech was the standard one of the Whigs during the campaign — that the administration favored the rich and disregarded the poor — but the variations were his own. In opposing the protective tariff, he said, the administration espoused the doctrine that "the wages of American labor must be brought down to the level of those of Europe." In establishing the subtreasury system the administration lowered both wages and prices and, that way, hurt the workingman while it helped the moneylending capitalist. "While his rich neighbor . . . is made richer . . . he, the honest and industrious mechanic, is crushed to earth; and yet we are told that this is a system for promoting the interests of the poor!" In attacking the banks the administration showed that it preferred gold coin, the aristocrat's money, "glittering through silk purses," to bank notes, the money of the common man.

The record, as Webster read it, showed the falsity of "the constant cry that the party of the administration is the true democratic party, or the more popular party." He denied the Democrats their claims to "democracy, in any constitutional sense." He appealed to "honest men not to take names for things, nor pretences for proofs." And then from the tariff and wages, banks and money, and the meaning of democracy he turned finally to the inevitable cabin and cider:

"But it is the cry and effort of the times to stimulate those who are called poor against those who are called rich; and yet, among those who urge this cry, and seek to profit by it, there is betrayed sometimes an occasional sneer at whatever savors of humble life. Witness the reproach against a candidate now before the people for their highest honors, that a log cabin, with plenty of hard cider, is good enough for him!

"Gentlemen, it did not happen to me to be born in a log cabin; but my elder brothers and sisters were born in a log cabin, raised amid the snowdrifts of New Hampshire, at a period so early that, when the smoke first rose from its rude chimney, and curled over the frozen hills, there was no similar evidence of a white man's habitation between it and the settlements on the rivers of Canada. Its remains still exist. I make to it an annual visit. I carry my children to it, to teach them the hardships endured by the generations which have gone before them. I love to dwell on the tender recollections, the kindred ties, the early affections, and the touching narratives and incidents, which mingle with all I know of this primitive family abode. I weep . . ."

And he wept sincerely. However irrelevant he may have been at the moment, he was always honestly sentimental about his family past.

Wherever he appeared, the party managers of the place put on a fitting popular demonstration for him. None was more elaborate than that in Boston, where on a bright September day thousands of horsemen, dozens of carriages containing graybeard Revolutionary veterans, and a long string of floats — a whaleboat from New Bedford, a colossal shoe from Lynn — paraded all the way from the Common to Bunker Hill, while from windows and balconies well-dressed women "with bright eyes and bounding bosoms" tossed bouquets. On Bunker Hill, Webster spoke briefly, then took refuge from a sudden shower by joining a few gentlemen at the home of one of them for some "cool, refreshing drinks."

Silas Wright, the administration rabble-rouser, following Webster from place to place to refute him and expose him as an aristocrat in disguise, was overmatched in the contest of demagoguery. At Patchogue, New York, the day before Wright was scheduled to speak there, Webster mimicked his voice and mannerisms, then shouted: "The man that calls me an aristocrat — is a LIAR!" A man who called him that, he added, "and then will not come within the reach of my arm, is not only a liar but a coward."

The Whig philosopher had become the Whig rabble-rouser. Along with his fellow partisans he adopted, till the votes were in, much of the Locofoco spirit. He emphasized, for the time being, the assumption that a real antagonism existed between the rich and the poor, the few and the many. But he directed against the Democrats themselves the class feeling they had fostered. *They,* he declaimed again and again and again, were the friends of the rich, *they* the enemies of the common man!

As Election Day approached, most of the Whigs rejoiced in what John J. Crittenden, writing to Webster from Kentucky, described as the "glorious excitement & uproar among the people." To Crittenden it seemed "a sort of popular insurrection in which patriotism, intelligence & good order" prevailed. But John Quincy Adams had his doubts. He wondered where the mass meetings and inflammatory harangues, the "revolution in the habits and manners of the people" would end. "Their manifest tendency is to civil war," he told his diary.

Whether or not the Whigs were running, as Adams implied, a serious risk that their democratic backfire against Democracy might get out of hand, the leaders of the party were at least to get their fingers burned as a result of the campaign tactics that led to victory in 1840.

V I
Fair Negotiation
1841-1844

"It has been wisely said, and it is true, that every settlement of national differences between Christian states by fair negotiation, without resort to arms, is a new illustration and a new proof of the benign influence of the Christian faith."

AT LAST, after March 4, 1841, Whigs could look hopefully ahead to four years in power. Looking beyond those four years, Daniel Webster was entitled to great expectations as he took over the State Department. In years gone by, one Secretary of State after another had succeeded to the presidency sooner or later.

True, Henry Clay had not, as yet. Clay now refused to take any place in the incoming cabinet. He intended to dominate the Harrison administration and to prepare his own candidacy for the next election from the Senate. So, from the outset, both Webster's aspirations and the party's program were jeopardized by a cutthroat rivalry between Webster and Clay.

From Harrison's election in November to his death the following April, the hapless old man found himself in the

middle of a tug of war between the two leading Whigs.
In the distribution of government jobs Webster did fairly
well. He not only got the highest appointive place for himself: he also worsted Clay in a contest over that sweetest
of patronage plums, the collectorship of the port of New
York. But he could not match Clay in influence among
his fellow cabinet appointees. After the inauguration
Clay won a majority to his side on the matter of calling
Congress for a special session at the end of May, his object
being to provide an official base from which to issue orders
to Harrison.

By the time Congress met, Harrison was in his grave
and Tyler in the White House. A Virginia gentleman,
with a gentleman's sense of personal honor, John Tyler
had a mind of his own, though it did not show in his out-
ward appearance, mild-mannered and slight of figure as he
was. He needed all his personal resources to deal with the
unprecedented situation. The first Vice President to take
over the presidential office, he held an uncertain status and
had no tradition to go by. He decided to assume Harrison's
title as well as his functions and to keep his cabinet.
Though not by choice, he also inherited all Clay's animos-
ity against Harrison.

Clay, as determined as ever to assert his mastery over
the party and the administration, schemed to push Tyler
into a corner where he would have no alternatives except
to submit or to leave the party. As the ground for a test of
strength Clay selected the issue of a national bank.
Throughout the spring and summer he pressed the issue.

Now, Tyler was willing to accept a national bank —
provided it conformed to his convictions with regard to
state rights. It would be constitutional, in his opinion, if it

беمنت

confined its operations primarily to the District of Columbia and established branches in the various states only with their consent. Webster did his best to maneuver the Tyler compromise, or something like it, through Congress.

But Clay was too much for him. Congress in September passed Clay's bill for a "fiscal corporation" which, despite the innocuous name, did not meet Tyler's objections to a national bank. Tyler vetoed it. Clay, to isolate him, called upon the cabinet members, as good Whigs, to resign. All did — except the Secretary of State.

Webster was up against one of the biggest dilemmas of his career. If he stayed with the administration, after all his fellow Whigs had left, he risked the loss of his party standing, even at home. Some New England Whigs, like John Quincy Adams, detested Tyler as a slaveholder and refused even to acknowledge him as quite their chief executive, always referring to him as the *acting* President of the United States. The manufacturers of Massachusetts, as two Lowell men told Adams, expected Tyler to deny them a new, high tariff and feared that Webster could or would do nothing to help. Most of Webster's constituents were dubious about the man in the White House.

Still, Webster hesitated to give up his office. It was the first administrative post he had ever held. He liked it, and he got along pleasantly with Tyler. He detested Clay and had no stomach for truckling to him. To stay might not necessarily lose Webster the support of his most important constituents; the businessmen of Boston agreed more with Tyler than with Clay on the question of the bank. Nathan Appleton had written a pamphlet opposing another institution like the Bank of the United States on the grounds that it would give too much power to one man and that

Massachusetts did not need it, with her highly efficient Suffolk System of interdependent state banks. If to some businessmen Webster seemed to be motivated by selfish politics rather than by concern for their interests, to others Clay seemed even more so.

Webster could not remain in office unless Tyler wanted to keep him. The President had the option of cutting loose entirely from the Whigs and trying to build up his strength among the Democrats, as his Virginia friends counseled him to do. But he might find it hard to attract those who condemned him as a renegade for having run on a Whig ticket. Perhaps, in partnership with Webster, he could construct a new middle party and steer a victorious course between Clayite and Jacksonian extremes.

"Where am I to go, Mr. President?" Webster asked Tyler, at the latter's White House desk, when the other secretaries had turned in their resignations. "You must decide that for yourself," Tyler replied. Seeing his opening, Webster quickly said: "If you leave it to me, Mr. President, I will stay where I am." Tyler rose and reached out his hand. "Give me your hand on that," he said, "and now I will say to you that Henry Clay is a doomed man from this hour."

Clay's doom, if doom it was, meant Webster's opportunity. After one or two terms for Tyler he could expect to be, himself, the candidate of the middle party. Meanwhile, as Secretary of State, he might infuse political vigor into the Tyler-Webster combination through his conduct of foreign affairs.

2

A third war between the United States and Great Britain seemed almost inevitable in 1842. There were serious points of conflict between the two countries. Both claimed several thousand square miles of land between New Brunswick and Maine; for nearly sixty years they had been unable to agree upon the location of the boundary as defined at the end of the Revolutionary war. Other border troubles followed the outbreak of the Canadian insurrection of 1837, during which the *Caroline,* an American boat carrying supplies to the rebels, was sunk in the Niagara River and an American citizen killed. The two governments wrangled also over questions of the slave trade and the freedom of the seas, questions which were exacerbated when British authorities in the West Indies seized the coastal slaver *Creole* and liberated its cargo.

In the United States the martial spirit waxed strong during the winter of 1841-1842, stronger on the frontier than in the seaport cities, stronger among the poor than among the well-to-do, stronger among Democrats than among Whigs. Expressing the Anglophobia of the time, a convention of Ohioans sent to the Secretary of State their resolutions calling upon him to press every American grievance "to the last extremity," that is, to the point of war.

But Webster had no such intention. The business community, especially that of Boston, was neither warlike nor anti-British. Still recovering from the panic of '37, and profiting from their economic connections with England,

most businessmen believed that their prosperity depended
on continued peace. And Webster himself inclined toward
appeasement of both American business and the British
government. He welcomed the task of putting Anglo-
American relations on a new and happier basis and, at the
same time, winning for himself and the Tyler administration the blessedness that presumably would attach to
peacemakers.

He got his opportunity when the incoming British min-
istry, itself peaceably disposed, sent Alexander Baring,
Lord Ashburton, on a treaty-making mission to the United
States. Ashburton, however, was not authorized to deal
with all the subjects in dispute. On the most urgent of
them, that of the northeastern boundary, he had instructions which would complicate Webster's task. He was to
compromise, but only on a basis that would assure his
government a feasible military route from Quebec to Hali-
fax, the better to fight the United States in case of a repe-
tition of the War of 1812.

The State of Maine, which (with Massachusetts)
claimed the whole of the disputed territory, was dead set
against any such compromise. Before Webster could pro-
ceed to negotiate with Ashburton, he had to win the
Maine commissioners to a partition of their state.

He did this with a secret weapon, his afterwards famous
"red-line map." He knew that at Paris, in 1783, Benjamin
Franklin had marked a map with a red line to indicate
the boundary, but no official copy was to be found in the
American archives. The American copy, like the British
and the Spanish, would have shown that Maine and the
United States were entitled to practically all the territory
they claimed. Webster did not know this, and he did not

care. He got hold of another map, an unofficial one. On it his friend Jared Sparks of Harvard drew a red line from his memory of a map which he had seen in the French archives and which he supposed to be the original. The line, as Sparks drew it, conceded the bulk of the British claim. This map suited the purposes of Webster, and he let the Maine commissioners have a look at it. They decided to accept a compromise.

Having accomplished this "grand stroke," as he afterwards called it, Webster was ready to talk with Ashburton. The two were not strangers. Ashburton was a partner in the firm of Baring Brothers, one of the great English banking houses, with heavy investments in American state bonds. Webster had been in the pay of Baring Brothers, who had looked to him for advice on ways and means to make good the bonds which several of the states had defaulted after the panic of '37. In the summer of 1842 Webster and Ashburton, plenipotentiaries for their respective governments, met in negotiations of the most informal and cozy sort, with nothing to try their tempers except the inevitable Washington heat.

After several weeks they produced a treaty and an exchange of notes. The treaty divided the disputed territory, awarding the United States somewhat more than half. It also provided for the extradition of criminals from Canada to the United States and for co-operation between the British and American navies in the suppression of the African slave trade. It did not so much as mention the cases of the *Caroline* or the *Creole,* the most serious grievances of the West and the South. These matters were discussed in the Webster-Ashburton correspondence, but this did not have the binding significance of the treaty itself.

In the Senate, where even the best of treaties were vulnerable to sectional and partisan attack, Webster might have expected rough going. His treaty was open to criticism both because of what it included and because of what it left out. On this issue Clay Whigs and Benton Democrats might unite against the administration. Behind the closed doors of the secret session, Senator Benton did denounce the treaty as sacrificing the interests of the West and the South to those of the Northeast, and some of his colleagues seconded his denunciations. But the redline map, which Webster, through Tyler, had transmitted to the Senate along with the treaty and the correspondence, exerted on most of the senators an effect as persuasive as on the Maine commissioners. Only nine voted against the treaty as the Senate gave its advice and consent to ratification.

Webster had completed but a part of his self-imposed task. If the treaty was to be a political asset, he needed the approval also of the American people.

Months earlier he had begun a propaganda campaign. With seventeen thousand dollars of State Department secret-service funds at his disposal, he hired F. O. J. ("Fog") Smith — an unscrupulous adventurer in journalism, business, politics, and love — to serve as a go-between with newspaper editors in Maine, where the greatest popular opposition had to be overcome. Smith made "certain assurances" to "a few individuals at different points in this state," in order to "adjust the tone and direction of the party presses and through them of public sentiment." The most influential of the Democratic "party presses" in Maine, and the only one with a considerable circulation outside the state, was the *Eastern Argus* of Portland. After

Smith got in touch with its editor, this newspaper ceased its diatribes against a boundary compromise and, in its own words, "entered heartily into the work of bringing about an honorable settlement."

During the negotiations Webster also had access to one of the nation's most often quoted sources of news and opinion, the *National Intelligencer* at Washington. Whig in outlook, but not the official organ of the Tyler administration, the *National Intelligencer* pretended to speak with detachment and impartiality. One of its publishers, however, was a close friend of Webster's, and Webster enjoyed the privilege of writing his own editorials and placing them unsigned in its columns. He also dropped hints to the Washington correspondents of some of the New York and Philadelphia papers.

He did not have everything his own way. The New York *Courier and Enquirer,* an organ of the Clay Whigs, and the Washington *Globe,* the voice of the Benton Democrats, found nothing good to say about his diplomacy. Ashburton and his banker friends, the *Globe* insisted, were going to bribe Webster into obligating the Federal government to pay off the defaulted state bonds that British financiers held. Though the *Globe* had its following in Maine and in other states, many Democratic as well as Whig editors professed to be shocked by "its appeals to the prejudices, passions, and fears of the people" and its injection of "party madness" into foreign affairs.

Throughout the country the *Eastern Argus,* the *National Intelligencer,* and the metropolitan papers carrying Webster's hints were much more often quoted than the central organs of the Clay Whigs and the Benton Democrats. By the time the treaty went to the Senate, newspaper

readers were generally prepared to believe what Webster
wished them to. The principal themes of his propaganda
were, first, that the treaty would dispose of all the trouble-
some issues with Great Britain in a way highly advanta-
geous to the United States and, second, that regardless of
the actual terms, the American people had no choice but
to accept them or face the prospect of a calamitous war.

After the Senate had acted on the treaty, Webster proceeded with his plans for its final reception by the public.
He intended, before revealing the terms themselves, to
publish three other items: the news of the Senate's over-
whelming vote, the correspondence with Ashburton cover-
ing some of the gaps in the treaty, and the message to the
Senate he had composed for Tyler, making the correspondence appear to be an authoritative and binding supple-
ment to the treaty itself. In short, he meant to administer
the antidote before the poison.

In the first of these steps he succeeded well enough. A
note he dashed off on the night of the Senate vote, "The
work is done — 39 to 9," appeared promptly in the *National Intelligencer,* which pointed the desired moral:
"When we consider the variety of subjects that the treaty
is supposed to embrace . . . this strong and decisive majority . . . gives the fullest assurance that the National
Honor has been maintained." Then, a few days later, a
news leak occurred that Webster had not intended. The
New York *Courier and Enquirer,* always alert to the best
interests of Clay, came out with the complete text of the
treaty. Thus the treaty "got before the public surrepti-
tiously," as Webster afterwards complained.

Yet he could hardly have arranged deliberately a better
timing for the release of news about its actual provisions.

At the opportune moment a tariff bill happened to pass the House of Representatives. Many Democratic editors, who previously had led their readers to expect a thorough and satisfactory settlement with England, now tacitly confirmed their predictions by slighting the treaty while denouncing the tariff.

Though some newspapers, Whig and Democratic, described the physical appearance of the document — "bound in crimson velvet, with ribbons to tie the covers together" — few of them bothered to detail its less colorful contents. Most of them accepted the alternatives that Webster anonymously had put forth: this particular agreement and peace, or its rejection and a disastrous war. Disregarding its omissions and inclusions, they endorsed it simply as an instrument of peace.

Whigs in the commercial centers of New England and the Middle states were the most enthusiastic. The Whig businessman's weekly digest of the news, *Niles' Register,* only reflected the predominant opinion of its many exchanges when it reminded its readers of the "awful consequences" of a war with England and hailed the treaty as a "harbinger of better times." Even the Clayite *Courier and Enquirer* finally gave grudging approval to the settlement as the best that could be had. Antislavery leaders, who feared at first that the extradition article might be misused for the recovery of fugitive slaves from Canada, were reassured by Ashburton himself. Southern planters, preoccupied with the sluggishness of the cotton market, generally welcomed the prospect of peaceful trade relations with England, the chief buyer of their crop. In the West similar considerations of peace and prosperity prevailed, despite the invective of such Western Democrats as

Benton and Lewis Cass, who continued to excoriate Webster and his handiwork. If, as Webster told Adams, Cass "thought to make great political headway upon a popular gale," he must have found the going rather hard.

Such wind as Webster's diplomacy and propaganda had stirred up was blowing with the President and the Secretary of State.

3

Popular though it was, the pact of peace with England did not arouse enough political force to advance Webster's ship very far, and shortly after its conclusion he had to deal with a mutiny. The ringleader was Abbott Lawrence, the prominent manufacturer, "the most leading man of Whig politics in Boston." As Adams noted, Lawrence had been "for many years devoted to Mr. Webster, and the main pillar of his support, both pecuniary and political." A "misunderstanding" between the two had begun a few years earlier, when Lawrence went for Clay in 1840 and Webster "coalesced with Harrison" against him. More recently, as one of the Massachusetts commissioners for the northeastern boundary arrangement, Lawrence felt that he deserved more credit than Webster allowed him for the final compromise. Now more than ever a devoted Clayite, Lawrence presided at a convention of Massachusetts Whigs who, in September 1842, proclaimed a "full and final separation" between themselves and Tyler and endorsed Clay for 1844.

So Webster had to choose between Lawrence and Tyler,

Boston and Washington, financial dependence and political ambition. If he chose Tyler, he would have to sacrifice much of the pecuniary support that Lawrence and others had given him in the past. Already they were denying him the usual favors, according to the gossip of Boston Democrats, one of whom, the historian-politician George Bancroft, told Van Buren: "The manufacturers no longer accept his drafts; the other day one was dishonored." On September 30, two days after Bancroft imparted this information, Webster gave his answer to the Massachusetts Whigs at a public meeting which, through some of his still loyal Boston friends, he had called in Faneuil Hall.

"I have had a hard summer's work," he told the assembled Whigs. "But if the results of my efforts shall be approved by the community, I am richly compensated." War between Christian states, he said, was contrary to "the judgment of civilization, of commerce, and of the heavenly light that beams over Christendom." In the late negotiations with England, he persuaded himself, he had shown "a proper regard for the preservation of peace between us and the greatest commercial nation of the world." He had stayed in Tyler's cabinet, he intimated, in order to carry through this great work of advancing business interests while maintaining the national honor.

But he gave no hint that, now the great work was done, he would resign. "I am, gentlemen, a little hard to coax, but as to being driven, that is out of the question." He defied the Whigs who would unwhig him. "I am a Whig, I have always been a Whig, and I always will be one; and if there are any who would turn me out of the pale of that communion, let them see who will get out first." He refused to disown the President, so long as Tyler continued to favor the interests of Massachusetts business and keep Massachusetts Whigs in Federal offices.

Then he turned from defense to attack, leveling his oratorical cannon at Clay and behind Clay, Lawrence, though he did not mention either man by name. He knew and everyone present was aware that Lawrence, the arch-protectionist of Boston, had done as much as anybody to lobby through Congress the recent law raising tariff rates. He also knew, as many in the audience apparently had forgotten, that his own tariff record since 1828 was more consistent than Clay's. He had opposed and Clay had sponsored the compromise of 1833 by which duties had been lowered year by year since then. "I may speak of the compromise act. My turn has come now," he gloated. At last he could say: I told you so. "The principle was bad, the measure was bad, the consequences were bad." And Clay, he implied, was to blame.

Considering all he had at hazard, this was one of the most independent and courageous performances that Webster ever gave. "Webster looked like Coriolanus," reported one of his least sympathetic hearers, the young and idealistic Charles Sumner. "He seemed to scorn, while he addressed, the people." Though the hall was "crowded to suffocation" the applause was light "and in rapture and spontaneousness was very unlike the echoes" he had excited in the same hall at other times. "We are all uncertain still whether he means to resign," Sumner said. And sour old John Quincy Adams characterized the speech as not only "ambiguous" but also "boastful, cunning, jesuitical, fawning, and insolent." Its only motive, Adams surmised, was "to propitiate the Democracy, and to split up the Whigs and out of the two fragments to make a Tyler party."

Even Webster's closest friends among the Whigs were perplexed by his bold apologia. "It is a *great* speech," Philip Hone in New York conceded to his diary, "but it will throw the whole Whig party into confusion." Hone did his best to make excuses for his hero's seeming disregard of party interests. "The flood which has set in with a force so irresistible for Mr. Clay as the next candidate for the presidency can never convey Mr. Webster on its bosom to personal honour or political distinction," he explained. "Their pretensions being equal, the elevation of the one forbids that of the other." It was, "perhaps, unfortunate for the party."

Hone and his fellow merchants of New York held a reception for Webster several weeks later, on the afternoon of November 4, to thank him for his services to the country — and to them — in negotiating the treaty with Ashburton. "Whatever may be the opinion of Mr. Webster's Whig friends as to his political position," Hone now observed, "they cannot deny him the credit of being the main instrument in effecting this important measure, the value of which posterity will appreciate." Certainly the New York businessmen did not deny him credit. At the city hall the president of the Chamber of Commerce presented him their resolutions of thanks and then flattered him in an address. In the midst of the ceremonies, "by a pleasing coincidence," a hundred guns were fired from each of several places in New York to celebrate the news that Great Britain had ratified the treaty.

That evening Webster dined at the Astor House with "a select knot of four-and-twenty Whigs," business leaders of the metropolis. "His expressive eyes shone with unusual lustre from under the dark canopy of his overhanging brows," or so it seemed to the impressionable Hone "and his brilliancy pervaded the whole table." After dinner, without rising, he talked for an hour — "in a plain, businesslike, colloquial strain, but in language pure as the dew of heaven" — about his late negotiations, telling how he and Ashburton had gone right to their task "like men of business." Then, confidentially, he rationalized in terms of partisan and business interests his remaining with the administration. He thought it better, he said, to "make the best of existing circumstances" and keep "patriotic Whigs" in charge of foreign affairs than to "throw the Executive bodily into the arms" of the Democrats.

For the moment, Hone believed, Webster had "recovered much of the ground he lost by his late speech at Faneuil Hall." But only for the moment, if that long. As the weeks passed he continued to lose popularity among Whigs and, largely because of that, he also lost his influence over the President. By winter's end in 1843, as he confessed to Biddle, he no longer had a say in the awarding of patronage even within his own department. Tyler, making "terrible" appointments, seemed "quite disposed to throw himself altogether into the arms of the loco foco party."

Webster was becoming embarrassed not only about the patronage but also about the Texas question. Antislavery Whigs suspected that Tyler was promoting a conspiracy to annex Texas and conquer California and thereby curry favor with expansionists, especially those of the South. Calling at the State Department (March 25, 1843), Adams accused Webster of abetting this slaveholders' plot. "Webster said I was wrong in all this," Adams recorded. But Adams was hard to convince, and he stayed to argue for three hours.

Webster explained to Adams that he had a scheme of

his own, which he had discussed with Tyler and with Ash-burton, both of whom had seemed agreeable to it. He intended to negotiate a three-way swap among Mexico, Great Britain, and the United States. Mexico would cede to the United States the northern part of California, including San Francisco Bay. The United States would yield to Great Britain its claims to Oregon north of the Columbia River. And Great Britain would give Mexico a sum of money with which Mexico could pay her debts to English and American creditors. This arrangement, Webster apparently thought, would appease expansionists and draw attention away from the Texas controversy, at least for the time being.

Increasingly uncomfortable as the odd man in the Tyler cabinet, Webster at last was willing to step out, but not into private life. He wanted to go on a diplomatic mission to England, where he had been lionized on his visit in 1839, where he had taken fondly to the historic monuments and the well-kept countryside, and where he thought he now had work to do. There he might negotiate his Anglo-Mexican-American settlement and refurbish his fame as the great pacificator. But he could not get from Congress an appropriation for a special mission.

If he went to England in any official capacity, he would have to go as minister to the Court of St. James. Of course, a minister from the United States was already there — Webster's old and intimate friend Edward Everett — who would have to be moved tactfully out of the way. For a while Webster thought he might get rid of Everett by sending him to China.

For years China had refused to receive ambassadors from other countries or to permit foreigners any rights of residence or trade except at the port of Canton. Then, at the conclusion of the Opium War in 1842, Great Britain obtained additional privileges. American merchants in Canton, who previously had petitioned their home government to send an agent to make a commercial treaty, now renewed and intensified their demands. Boston and Salem merchants engaging in the China trade did the same. The famous medical missionary and chargé d'affaires in Canton, Dr. Peter Parker, had visited Washington in 1841 and impressed upon Webster the importance of an active policy in the Far East.

Responding to these pressures, Webster composed a message on relations with China for Tyler to transmit to the House of Representatives at the end of 1842. "It cannot but be important to the mercantile interest of the United States, whose intercourse with China at the single port of Canton has already become so considerable," Webster wrote, "to ascertain whether these other ports, now open to British commerce, are to remain shut, nevertheless, against the commerce of the United States." Not that he exaggerated the potentialities of the Chinese market, as many Americans were afterward to do. He conceded that "the cheapness of labor among the Chinese" and "the fixed character of their habits" might "discourage the hope of the opening of any great and sudden demand for the fabrics of other countries." But, he pointed out, American exports to China had doubled during the previous ten years and could be expected to go on increasing if new ports were made accessible. The "commercial interests of the United States," he said, "require vigilance." He recommended sending a commissioner to negotiate a treaty and to reside in China.

When Adams introduced a bill (in February 1843) to

appropriate forty thousand dollars for such a mission, Senator Benton attacked it as a trick to get Webster to London, but few of his colleagues took him seriously. The bill passed, but the trick failed. At the Court of St. James, Minister Everett, complaining that he had scarcely warmed his seat, declined to budge.

Webster then secured the appointment of his friend and creditor Caleb Cushing for the China trip. Before drawing up instructions for Cushing, Webster distributed a circular to the China traders of Boston and Salem asking them for suggestions. He composed also a letter to the Manchu emperor from the President of the United States. This missive, which was not one of Webster's great state papers, read like a communication to the chief of some Indian tribe. In China, Cushing faithfully handed the message to a representative of the emperor and, though not because of it, obtained from him (in the Treaty of Wanghia, 1844) a guarantee that the emperor would extend to the United States the same privileges as to the most favored nation.

By that time Webster was out of office. He could derive such satisfaction as he would from the knowledge that he had carried through one and set afoot another diplomatic enterprise to promote American prosperity. He could also derive such satisfaction as he would from Tyler's continuing good will, expressed at the end in Tyler's gracious acceptance of his resignation. These satisfactions were, at best, small compensation for the collapse of the political hopes he had taken with him into the State Department.

4

If between them Webster and Tyler had succeeded in making a middle party go, it might have eased some of the sectional strains which were to culminate in civil war. When he and Tyler parted, the middle ground where moderates might rally was narrowed.

To his cabinet place came the proslavery Abel P. Upshur of Virginia and then the even more rabidly proslavery John C. Calhoun of South Carolina. Tyler having declared for immediate Texas annexation, Calhoun coupled it with the slavery cause by demanding it frankly as a means of protecting and preserving the peculiar institution of the South. There was no compromising with Calhoun.

Neither Calhoun nor Tyler, for all their annexationist enthusiasm, got the Democratic nomination in 1844. Nor did Van Buren, the preconvention favorite who tried to evade the Texas question. Instead, the dark horse James K. Polk ran on the twin slogans of the "reannexation" of Texas and the "reoccupation" of Oregon, slogans designed to please the South and appease the North. The Whigs nominated their party master Henry Clay, who like Van Buren straddled the territorial issue.

Webster, having returned to the party fold, dutifully stumped the State of Pennsylvania, where he warned protectionist Democrats that Polk was an antitariff man. On the Texas question he spoke out forthrightly to oppose annexation because it "would tend to prolong the duration and increase the extent of African slavery on this continent." Sticking to the subjects of Texas and the tariff, he said as little as possible about the Whig candidate himself. Once the returns were in, Clay had no chance to show how he would have rewarded him.

VII

Example of a Republic
1845–1848

"I have always wished that this country should exhibit to the nations of the earth the example of a great, rich, and powerful republic which is not possessed by a spirit of aggrandizement."

THE BIG BUSINESSMEN of Boston and New York trembled at the prospect of four years under such a president as James K. Polk. To them he seemed likely to prove as bad as Tyler, Van Buren, or even Jackson in his domestic program and worse than any of the three in his foreign policies. Now as never before the businessmen had need of an able champion to fight at least a delaying action for them in the Senate.

Before Polk's inauguration the Whigs in the Massachusetts legislature recalled Daniel Webster from private life and elected him senator. But he doubted that he could or would accept the assignment. As usual he needed money. Some of his wealthy constituents, needing his services, took steps to provide it. "The project is to raise a fund of 100,000 dollars here & in N York, the income to be settled on him & his wife for life, reversion to ye subscribers," Harrison Gray Otis wrote privately from Boston (February 7, 1845). "This is at least the third time that the wind has been raised for him, and the most curious fact is that thousands are subscribed by many who hold his old notes for other thousands, and who have not been backward in their censures of his profusion."

Otis himself was not a subscriber this time — "not able to be one," he said — and neither was Abbott Lawrence. While the subscription list was being circulated, Webster through Nathan Appleton made overtures to Lawrence for patching up their broken friendship. "All Webster's political systems are interwoven with the exploration of a goldmine for himself," the puritanical John Quincy Adams noted when he heard of these personal negotiations, "and all his confidential intimacies with Lawrence have been devices to screw from him or, by his agency, from others money by the fifty or hundred thousand dollars at a time." Though Lawrence agreed to forget his quarrel with Webster, he still declined to subscribe. Forty other Boston businessmen, however, contributed.

So Webster went on to Washington to join the Senate and oppose the administration. But the financial arrangement which made his presence possible soon jeopardized his effectiveness by making him vulnerable to partisan attack.

He would have run into criticism anyhow on account of his record as Secretary of State. Congressmen and senators accused him of having abandoned American rights in Maine and having stultified American claims to Oregon. Then, in the House, Charles J. Ingersoll, a Democrat from Pennsylvania, undertook to impeach him retroactively for "fraudulent misapplication and personal use of the public funds." Ingersoll specified that Webster, while secretary, had used secret-service money for "corrupting party presses" in Maine and had been, and still was, more than two thousand dollars short in his accounts with the government. With self-righteous fury Webster "grit his teeth, scowled, stamped, and roared forth" against his accuser, whom he referred to as "a man or a thing" and finally disposed of thus: "I now leave the gentleman — I leave him with the worst company I know on the face of the earth — I leave him with himself." Four members of a five-man investigating committee in the House exonerated Webster from impeachable offenses but refused to publish the whole of the evidence.

The impeachment charges set off a House debate on the public morals of the senator whom many Whigs worshiped as the "Godlike Daniel." After listening to a eulogy from an Alabama Whig, the Alabama Democrat William L. Yancey launched a philippic far more damaging then Ingersoll's tirade. What, Yancey asked, entitled "this illustrious and godlike personage" to his fame? Was it his obstruction of the War of 1812, his advice to the Baring bank on the collectibility of state debts ("an opinion given to a foreign Jew money-lender against his own countrymen"), or his sacrifice of his country's interests in the Ashburton treaty?

"I have been informed that the sum of $100,000 has been raised by the friends of Mr. Webster, to pension him as a Senator of the United States," said Yancey, coming to the gravamen of his case. "If he is paid, what is it for? Is it that his eloquent voice may merely resound within the walls of the Senate chamber? Is it that he may adorn the public counsels merely, without any view to private and personal interests? That is not human nature."

Representative Robert C. Winthrop, from Massachusetts, rose to deny that Webster was "in any just sense, the pensioned agent of the manufacturing interest." Winthrop averred: "He is here as no agent of private individuals. He holds his seat by the free and unsolicited suffrages of the Legislature of Massachusetts." Members of that legislature had sent him to the Senate because they believed that he would advance the best interests "not merely of their own fellow-citizens" but also of "the whole people of the Union." The recent gift to Webster was a "private transaction," of no public concern.

Yancey, on his feet again, insisted that it was a "transaction involving public character and morals," and he contrasted Webster's public character with that of other men in Congress. The "venerable gentleman" from Massachusetts, John Quincy Adams, when presented with a "splendid Bible," had told the donors "that *he* could not thus receive it" and had paid them "its value of $20." A "distinguished son of Kentucky," John J. Crittenden, had "had a splendid farm offered him for public services rendered," but "*he* could not, with his high sense of propriety, and of the delicate relations of a public man to the people, accept of such a present!" Webster, despite his "great intellectual name," possessed no such "public integrity" as that. "Mr. Webster has two characters, which Proteus-like he can assume as his interests or necessities demand — the 'God-like' and the 'Hell-like' — the 'God-like Daniel' and *'Black Dan'!*"

To this charge Webster did not reply.

2

For value received, Webster provided loyal if futile services to his generous constituents during the Polk administration. These businessmen were modest enough in what
they wanted from the Federal government. They wanted
to see things kept pretty much as they already were, the
tariff of 1842 unchanged, the subtreasury system (repealed during the Whig interlude under Tyler) forgotten, the nation at peace, its boundaries fixed. But Polk had
taken office with a program which ran counter to their
desires. He aimed to undo the tariff, re-establish an independent treasury, and annex not only Texas but also Oregon and California. He was to risk war with England,
provoke war with Mexico, and prepare the way for war
within the United States.

In resisting the presidential program Webster gained a
point only where Polk was willing to concede one, on the
Oregon question. When the President threatened to
carry out the campaign slogan of "Fifty-four forty or
fight," the Michigan Democrat Lewis Cass proposed to his
Senate colleagues that they look into the military defenses
of the United States, and he meant that they get ready for
war with England. Webster, answering Cass, deplored the
"unnecessary alarm and apprehension" which the administration was arousing. Businessmen owned "immense
amounts of property" afloat and ashore, he said, and even
a rumor of war would "affect the value of that property."
With the co-operation of Calhoun he secured the passage
of a Senate resolution which led to a compromise with

England, a division of the Oregon country along the forty-ninth parallel.

While the administration tariff bill was in the making, Webster called upon the Boston manufacturers to aid him in preparing a case against it. "We shall need the advice of our best informed & most prudent friends," he wrote to Nathan Appleton. Let us "hear from you & your neighbors as fully as possible. It would be very well, I think, if some intelligent Gentlemen from Boston could spend the next ten days in Washington." From both manufacturers and shipowners he gathered facts and figures to show how their interests would suffer under the proposed schedule of duties. For all his speechmaking and his friends' lobbying, however, he could not defeat or even significantly revise the administration's bill, which became the Walker Tariff in 1846.

Likewise he was powerless to defeat the independent treasury bill, denounce it though he did for "its strange, un-American character," its spirit of antagonism toward the "commercial community." And he could not persuade the Senate to override Polk's veto of the river and harbor bill of 1846, which would have committed the Federal government to internal improvements on a considerable scale.

Equally forlorn was his opposition to Polk's plans for territorial aggrandizement. Nevertheless he spoke and voted against the admission of Texas as a state and against the declaration of war with Mexico. Once the war had begun, he gave a qualified support to its prosecution, confiding to his son Fletcher: "We may think a war unnecessary or unjust; but if a majority think otherwise, we must submit, because we have agreed that a majority shall govern."

He acquired a more personal reason for not trying to withhold supplies from the Army when his younger son Edward went to Mexico as a captain of Massachusetts Volunteers. Just as the war was ending, and only a few weeks after Webster's daughter, Mrs. Samuel Appleton, had succumbed to tuberculosis, Edward sickened and died in Mexico, leaving Webster childless except for Fletcher.

While sustaining the soldiers who, obedient to duty's call, were "upholding the flag of the country," Webster condemned Polk for having maneuvered the country into war in the first place. There had been, he said, no danger of attack from Mexico at the time Polk ordered Zachary Taylor's troops into disputed territory along the Rio Grande, thus "naturally, if not necessarily, tending to provoke hostilities" on the part of the Mexicans. "No power but Congress can declare war; but what is the value of this constitutional provision, if the President of his own authority can make such military movements as must bring on war?"

Braving obloquy as a "Mexican Whig," Webster demanded that the war be brought to an early end — but not on Polk's terms. The President intended to buy peace and, with it, half of Mexico. When he asked Congress for the necessary appropriation, he ran into difficulties with Democrats as well as Whigs. Some Northern members of his party felt that by taking all of Texas and only part of Oregon the President had favored the South and slavery and slighted the North and free soil. They balked when he now appeared to seek a still further extension of slave territory. One of them, Representative David Wilmot of Pennsylvania, tried to amend the appropriation bill with a proviso that slavery be prohibited everywhere in territory to be acquired from Mexico.

The Wilmot Proviso did not go far enough to suit Webster. He wanted to avoid the whole controversial subject by preventing the acquisition of any new territory at all. "The country is already large enough," he said. Though he voted for the Wilmot Proviso, he preferred the alternative which a Georgia Whig offered, the Berrien amendment, disavowing territorial conquest as a war aim. But the "Northern Democracy" and the "Southern Democracy" agreed, as Webster put it, "to carry on the war for territory, though it be not decided now whether the character of newly acquired territory shall be that of freedom or of slavery." This point they were "willing to leave for future agitation and future controversy."

Webster frankly mentioned the tariff as one reason for his stand against new annexations. He reminded his colleagues that after the admission of Texas as a state in December 1845, two additional senators had appeared in Washington. "In July, 1846, these two Texan votes turned the balance in the Senate and overthrew the tariff of 1842, in my judgment the best system of revenue ever established in this country." In the future the tariff question would come up again, and no doubt at the "suitable time," if necessary, two senators from California or New Mexico would "make their appearance here." And, later on, another pair from Sonora, another from Tamaulipas, and still others from such additional provinces as might be taken from Mexico!

After California and New Mexico had become American territories despite Webster's vote against the treaty of peace, he steadily resisted every step toward making proslavery and antitariff states out of them. The Senate concentrated its attention first on the creation of a territorial government for Oregon, and Stephen A. Douglas of Illi-

nois proposed extending westward to the Pacific the line
of the Missouri Compromise (slavery in the Lousiana
Purchase south but not north of 36° 30′). The Douglas
amendment would have guaranteed free soil in the Oregon Territory, but it did not appease free-soilers in the
Senate. "The truth is," Webster pointed out, "that it is an
amendment by which the Senate wishes to have now a
public, legal declaration, not respecting Oregon, but respecting the newly acquired territories of California and
New Mexico. It wishes now to make a line of slavery which
shall include those new territories."

The Douglas compromise did not satisfy the proslavery
senators from the South any more than it did the free-soil
senators from the North. Calhoun and others insisted that
under the Constitution slaveowners had a right to take
their property anywhere within the Federal domain.
"Their 'property'?" Webster inquired. He certainly would
not deny them the privilege of taking with them everything that "in the general estimate of human society" was
considered property. The real meaning of the Southerners' complaint, he said, was that they could not "go into
the territories of the United States carrying with them
their own peculiar local law, a law which creates property
in persons." So Webster, cheered on by his old party foe
Thomas Hart Benton, spoke like a true friend of freedom.

As Polk's term neared its end, there were so many ex-
tremists and so few compromisers in both the Senate
and the House that no territorial settlement was possible
for the time being. The President and his followers in
Congress had brought on a sectional crisis which they
left for another administration and another Congress to
dispose of.

3

In the time of Polk the reformist urges of Jacksonian Democracy broadened into nationalist demands for military conquest. Expansionism seemed a corollary of egalitarianism to Democratic intellectuals who rationalized the new trend. Conquest was "Manifest Destiny," a phrase coined by a party journalist in 1845. The United States had a divine mission to make room by force of arms for its yearly multiplying millions and, while so doing, to spread the blessings of democracy among less favored peoples who happened to occupy attractive lands nearby.

While demanding living space for democracy beyond the borders, the followers of Polk did not neglect the radical spirit of democracy at home which, as followers of Jackson, they formerly had avowed. Indeed, Polk's Secretary of the Treasury, Rober J. Walker, presented his plan for tariff reduction as a means of saving hapless workingmen from greedy capitalists and the nation as a whole from the terrors of class conflict.

"As the profit of capital invested in manufactures is augmented by the protective tariff," said Walker in an antiprotectionist manifesto, "there is a corresponding increase of power, until the control of such capital over the wages of labor becomes irresistible. As this power is exercised from time to time we find it resisted by combinations among the working classes by turning out for higher wages or for shorter time; by trades-unions; and in some countries unfortunately by violence and bloodshed. But the government by protective duties arrays itself on the side of the manufacturing system, and by thus augmenting its wealth and power soon terminates in its favor the struggle between man and man — between capital and labor."

To refute the ideas of the Polk administration, Webster brought his social and political philosophy up to date in private letters, political and occasional addresses, and legal arguments during the 1840's. He contended that Polk's ways, like Jackson's, rested on assumptions neither democratic nor "American." (He deserves such credit or blame as attaches to being the first to introduce the epithet *un-American* into political debate.) His own conception of the American way included the following postulates: class harmony realized through government aid to business enterprise, popular power based on wide diffusion of property ownership, Christianity as the essential basis for civil society, constitutional restrictions on majority rule, limitation of territorial growth, propagation of American ideals abroad by peaceful means, and technological progress as an automatic instrumentality for perfecting and extending the American way.

According to Webster the Democrats did an "extreme injustice" when they attacked the tariff as favoring "the rich corporations of New England." He said it favored the workingman just as much, for it would "induce capitalists to invest their capital in such a manner as to occupy and employ American labor." Free trade brought the working people to starvation, as in Ireland. Protection raised them to high living standards, made them "cheerful, contented, spirited," and "respectable," as in the United States. In the textile factories of New England "female operatives" cleared, after paying for their board, two dollars a week, and "male workmen" twelve dollars a month. Not only they but all their fellow citizens — sugar planters and cotton growers in the South, farmers everywhere — prospered under the beneficent influence of the tariff. So saying, Webster offered this credo: first, "that the tariff favors every interest in the country"; and, second, "that the manufacturing is not an exclusive but a general interest."

In other words, the Federal government by proper intervention in economic affairs could advance and reconcile all special interests by fostering one general interest: that of the Boston capitalists with their investments in textile mills. The United States could do still more for the general good by following the example — not of England, "where private enterprise and wealth have gone so far ahead," but of Russia, Prussia, Austria, Saxony, and Sardinia, where a "spirit of improvement" caused government to act. "We behold mountains penetrated by railroads, safe harbors constructed, everything done by government for the people which, in the nature of the case, the people cannot do for themselves."

In 1847, when a new edition of his works was being prepared, Webster still believed, as he had maintained in his address to the Massachusetts constitutional convention, "that it is dangerous to sever political power and property." He told the editor of his works: "I have been abused for the doctrines of this same speech, and I wish to defend it, *tandem,* in a note." In 1820 he had used the doctrine to justify free trade; in the 1840's he adapted it to his argument for the tariff. Under the business system, which the tariff stimulated, and under the laws of inheritance, property was distributed as fast as it was accumulated, he now believed. A "great division of property into small parcels" did in fact exist, "especially at the North," and to some degree even in the South. "Slave labor and rice and cotton cultivation," Webster wrote privately while on a visit to South Carolina (1847), "work in badly with democratic subdivisions of property, such as suit us in New England." Yet the abolition of primogeniture (after the Revolution) had "broken in upon the whole old-fashioned aristocratic system of Southern life."

Webster stated his views on Christianity and society when he presented his brief in the Girard will case (1844). The Philadelphia merchant Stephen Girard had left his fortune for endowing an orphan school from which religious teachings and clergymen of whatever kind were to be forever excluded. Some of the disappointed Girard heirs attempted to break the will. Taking their case, Webster argued that the devise was *"no charity at all"* because it was "derogatory to the Christian religion," and "the Christian religion, its general principle, must ever be regarded among us as the foundation of civil society." He lost the case but won the applause of many conservatives.

He analyzed the conservative features of "our *glorious* representative system of popular government" in another legal brief. The case of *Luther* v. *Borden,* which the Supreme Court decided in 1848, had grown out of the Dorr rebellion in Rhode Island several years earlier. Led by Thomas L. Dorr, an extralegal convention of Rhode Islanders had set aside the existing state constitution (the original colonial charter, little changed), which contained high property qualifications for voting and holding office. The Dorrites adopted a new, more democratic constitution and operated a state government under it until the forces of established law and order dispersed them. Martin Luther, a shoemaker and an official of the Dorr government, then sued Luther Borden, an agent of the established order, for housebreaking. Luther's case against Borden depended on the constitutional validity of the Dorr government.

In Borden's behalf Webster contended that the Dorr proceedings had created not government but "anarchy," and tended not toward constitutional freedom but toward "a tumultuary, tempestuous, violent, stormy liberty." On the other hand, the proceedings of the charter government offered nothing to complain of, "except that it might perhaps have discreetly taken measures at an earlier period for revising the constitution. If in that delay it erred, it was the error into which prudent and cautious men would fall." Those prudent and cautious men had followed the American political tradition, as Webster viewed it. "From 1776 to the latest period the whole course of American public acts, the whole progress of this American system," he said, "was marked by a peculiar conservatism."

He conceded that American government was based upon the will of the people, but he insisted that the people must express their will through the procedures they already had approved. In their constitutions they had agreed to *limit themselves.*" They had secured their government against "the sudden impulses of mere majorities," against "hasty changes by simple majorities," in obedience to "their great conservative principle."

After winning his case for Borden, Webster the next year elaborated some of the themes of his brief in an address before a festival of the Sons of New Hampshire in Boston. Self-government and the enjoyment of equal rights, he then said, were practicable so long as men remembered that "freedom from restraint is not FREEDOM" and that a "general scramble which leads the idle and the extravagant to hope for a time when they may put their hands into their neighbors' pockets, call it what you please, is tyranny. It is no matter whether the Sultan of Turkey robs his subject of his property or whether, under the notion of equal rights, the property earned by one shall be taken from him by a majority."

Webster thus shared some of the fear of what Calhoun called the tyranny of the majority, yet saw no need for Calhoun's drastic remedy of nullification. So far as Webster was concerned, the existing representative system provided security enough for men of property so long as the system was properly understood and applied, and so long as property was widely distributed.

Neither the representative system nor the harmony of group interests could be preserved, according to Webster, if the American government extended its sway over a large and diverse empire. The Constitution, he said in a Senate speech on the Mexican War, was designed to make the people of the United States *"one people,* one in interest, one in character, and one in political feeling. If we depart from that, we break it all up." And if we tried to incorporate peoples like the Mexicans, utterly different from us in morals and manners, we would depart from that principle of unity. "Arbitrary governments may have territories and distant possessions, because arbitrary governments may rule them by different laws and different systems. Russia may rule in the Ukraine and the provinces of the Caucasus and Kamtschatka by different codes, ordinances, or ukases. We can do no such thing. They must be of us, *part* of us, or else strangers."

Although Webster thus repudiated the Manifest Destiny

of the Democrats, he preached another kind of American Destiny, a warless one, through which Americans and Englishmen hand in hand would eventually inherit the earth. Big with prophecy, he told the New England Society of New York (1843): "I can only see that on this continent *all* is to be *Anglo-American* from Plymouth Rock to the Pacific seas, from the north pole to California." And Anglo-American hegemony would not end there. "If there be anything in the supremacy of races, the experiment now in progress will develop it," he went on. "If there be any truth in the idea that those who issued from the great Caucasian fountain, and spread over Europe, are to react on India and on Asia . . ." For himself, he believed that the "progress and dominion of the favored races" had no limit. Englishmen and Americans — "these branches of a common race" — would win the world for the white man through the invincible virtue of their principles: *"the freedom of thought and the respectability of individual character."*

After the Mexican War, Webster continued to preach a sort of cultural expansionism. He expected the American way to spread to other countries gradually and peaceably through the influence of changing technology. Other countries could not remake themselves overnight, however. When the revolutionary movements of 1848 shook Europe, he was dubious about the probable results, especially in France. "We are in an age of progress," he declared. "That progress is towards self-government by the enlightened portion of the community, everywhere." But progress could not be hastened by violence, he warned. "It is a common sentiment, uttered by those who would revolutionize Europe, that to be free men have only to *will* it. That is a fallacy." We ourselves, we who were "an offshoot of the British constitution," had learned self-government "only by an experience of two hundred years." Our example and our experience would in time affect Europe as a result of mechanical developments. "We are brought by steam, and the improvements attendant upon its discovery, into the immediate neighborhood of the great powers of Europe, living under different forms of government." And "this bringing the republican practice into the immediate presence of despotism, monarchy, and aristocracy" was bound to have an effect.

At home as well as abroad the new technology was the great leveler, the great harmonizer, the bringer of social happiness as well as material comfort. Webster could not find praise enough for "this mighty agent, steam." As he said at a reception in Savannah, Georgia (1847): "It lessens labor, it economizes time, it gives the poor man leisure and ability to travel, it joins the most remote regions and brings their inhabitants face to face, establishing a harmony of interest and feeling between them. It limits all distinctions. The poor and the rich, the prince and the peasant, enjoy now equal facilities of travel, and can procure the same comforts and luxuries from distant points, and when they travel they sit side by side in the same railcar. The individual is sinking, and the mass rising up in the majesty of a common manhood." In the utopian conservatism of Webster, mechanical invention could overcome class, sectional, and international conflicts if men would but encourage it and give it time.

4

The election of 1848, as Webster viewed it, brought into a new focus the clash of ideas between conservative and pacifist Whigs, on the one hand, and radical and war-like Democrats on the other. The election also brought him the usual fourth-year frustration and placed him in another of his quadrennial dilemmas.

Again he had failed to realize his hopes of running, and winning, as the Whig candidate. In 1847 he had gone South on what his friends considered an electioneering tour, but at convention time he received the support of few Southern Whigs and few Northern ones either, even in his own state. The Whig party in Massachusetts was breaking up over the issues raised by the Mexican War, the Conscience Whigs being inclined to oppose and the Cotton Whigs to appease the slaveholders of the South. Conscience Whigs were beginning to distrust Webster, despite his consistent free-soilism in the Senate, and Cotton Whigs could not agree among themselves about his presidential availability, willing though they had been to finance a senatorial career for him. Robert Winthrop, for one, "was decidedly of opinion that in the existing condition of public affairs the Democrats would win an easy victory should the Conservative nominee prove to be Clay, Webster, or Judge McLean." The "only chance for the Whigs," in Winthrop's judgment, was "to run an untried man," preferably one "whose name would excite popular sympathy outside of politics."

Remembering their success with a war hero in 1840,

the nation's Whigs finally nominated another one in 1848. Their candidate, General Zachary Taylor, victor of Buena Vista, owned slaves in Louisiana but never had made a controversial pronouncement on slavery, the territories, or any other public question. As Taylor's running mate, the convention was ready to name a Massachusetts man: Webster himself if he had been willing, or Abbott Lawrence if the Webster Whigs had not objected to him. As it was, they gave the vice-presidential nomination (and ultimately the presidency itself) to Millard Fillmore, of New York.

A victory for Taylor and the Whigs seemed more than doubtful as the campaign got under way. His Democratic opponent, Lewis Cass, having fought against the British in the War of 1812, could also claim something of a military reputation, and he had the power of the Polk administration behind him. A third party with a free-soil platform and a combined Democratic and Whig ticket — former President Martin Van Buren and John Quincy Adams's son Charles Francis Adams — threatened to draw more votes away from Taylor than from Cass. And, as if the Whig managers did not have worries enough, the golden voice of their godlike campaigner remained strangely mute as Election Day came nearer week by week.

Through that summer Webster struggled with his own disgust and doubt and indecision, recording the course of his thought in letters to his son Fletcher. "I shall endeavor to steer my boat with discretion." "And I can see no way but acquiescence in Taylor's nomination, not enthusiastic support nor zealous affection, but acquiescence or forbearance from opposition." "I must not, in consistency, abandon the support of Whig principles. My own reputation will not allow of this. I cannot be silent, without being reproached, when such as Cass is pressed upon the country." "The Whigs generally, & a good many Democrats, of *property*, will vote for Gen. T. to keep out Gen. C. — through fear that the latter will bring on *War* with some nation or another." "We can do no good by holding out. We shall only isolate ourselves." "I must say *something, somewhere*, soon —"

At last, on September 1, he said something. General Taylor, he began, was "a military man, and a military man merely," with "no training in civil affairs." The Whigs were "not wise nor discreet to go to the Army for the selection of a candidate for the Presidency of the United States." Himself, he would stand by the statement he had made at convention time, "that if General Taylor should be nominated by the Whig convention, fairly, I should not oppose his election." He still believed, however, that "such a nomination was not fit to be made."

He went on to explain that he considered Taylor, bad as his nomination was, to be less dangerous than the Democratic candidate. The country needed a President who would "not plunge us into further wars of ambition and conquest," who would not promote "the further extension of slavery in this community or its further influence in the public councils," and who would strive to bring about "an essential reform in the system of revenue and finance" which would restore prosperity by "fostering the labor of the country." Taylor appeared to be qualified in each of these respects.

"Now as to General Cass, Gentlemen." Cass had tried to defeat the Ashburton treaty and the Oregon settlement with England, and he "could have prevented the Mexican war" but had been "first and foremost in pressing that war." Though a better man than Polk, he was inclined to "rash politics" both at home and abroad. "He would consider himself not as conservative, not as protective to present institutions, but as belonging to the party of Progress. He believes in the doctrine of American destiny; and that that destiny is to go through wars and invasions and maintain vast armies to establish a great, powerful, domineering government over all this continent."

As for Van Buren, he and the rest of the Free Soil party were no better free-soilers than Webster himself, and many of them were worse, since they had voted for the annexation of Texas and the acquisition of additional lands from Mexico. So said Webster. "That the leader of the Free Spoil party should so suddenly have become the leader of the Free Soil party," he jibed, "would be a joke to shake his sides and mine."

In a Faneuil Hall stump speech, a week or two before Election Day, Webster spoke out again, and this time he tried to turn back upon the Democrats their Anglophobia and their class-consciousness.

"In my judgment, Gentlemen," he told the Whigs of Boston, "for a whole year back the rich have been growing richer and richer; the active and industrious classes have been more and more embarrassed; and the poor have been growing poorer and poorer, every day throughout the whole year. And in my judgment, further, so long as this sub-treasury lasts, so long as the present rate of duties and customs lasts, that is to say, so long as the tariff of 1846 continues, this state of accumulation by the rich, of distress of the industrious classes, and of the aggravated poverty of the poor, will go on from degree to degree, to an end which I shall not attempt to calculate." Here he was hinting that a revolutionary crisis might arrive unless the tariff should be restored and the independent treasury abolished.

The advocates of free trade and hard money, he went on, were also the critics of the Ashburton treaty and the Oregon settlement. "And one thing further strikes me — that, while there are of this school of politicians men whose views were heard in either house of Congress, and through the columns of all the newspapers, big with taunts, threats, and defiance to England, they are the men that, in all our own legislation upon tariffs and currency, act exactly the part that a British minister would most desire they should."

By coming out for the Whig candidate, Webster doubtless contributed something toward the victory at the polls, but his support was too late and too grudging to gain him much gratitude from Taylor and Taylor's friends. At a Boston dinner soon after the election Abbott Lawrence lauded the President-elect and vouched for his soundness as a Whig, and then Webster spoke up to rebuke the Massachusetts Whigs in much the same tone he had used with them on the occasion of his defiant Faneuil Hall appearance of 1842. The party of conservatism remained divided, not only because of sectional interests but also because of personal ambitions and differences of opinion about the demagogic use of military heroes.

V I I I
Exigent Interests
1849-1852

"Sir, there is no generation of mankind whose opinions are not subject to be influenced by what appears to them to be their present emergent and exigent interests."

İṄ THE WINTER of 1849-1850 the crisis came which Daniel Webster had prophesied would come if the United States should take any territory from Mexico. The new President, Zachary Taylor, for all the slaves he owned on his Louisiana plantation, demanded that Congress let California join the Union as a free state, and Southern hotheads swore that their own states would go out if California thus came in. Meanwhile, to expand the area of slavery, they backed the Texan imperialists who claimed much of New Mexico as a part of Texas. Over this boundary question a civil war seemed likely to break out, with Northerners rallying to the support of New Mexico and free soil.

To save the Union, the aging compromiser Henry Clay offered his last great compromise. Admit California with an antislavery constitution, he recommended, and settle the boundary dispute in favor of New Mexico. Do even more for the North: abolish the slave trade (though not slavery itself) in the District of Columbia. But compensate Texas by assuming her public debt, and reassure the South by passing a law more effective than the existing one for the capture and return of escaping slaves. Forget the Wilmot Proviso: say nothing about slavery in organizing the territories of New Mexico and Utah.

As between the plan of Taylor, who refused to consider tying California with the other issues, and the proposals of Clay for a general settlement, where would Webster stand?

Many antislavery people in the North hoped that he would stand with the cause of liberty. One of these people, a Unitarian preacher in Philadelphia, reminded him "how Slavery has *interfered* & is *interfering*, not with property, but with the rights, with the inmost hearts of freemen, making them its tools & supporters," and begged him to make "in that grand & simple way" of his a speech *"stating the great case."*

His friends the New York merchants also opposed concessions to the South, at first, but early in 1850 they changed their attitude. They feared the loss of their profitable Southern trade when Southerners began to talk of seceding or, even without secession, boycotting Northern goods. In February the merchants called a mass meeting of New Yorkers "irrespective of party" to demonstrate in favor of "sustaining Mr. Clay's compromise" as the best way of achieving "the permanent settlement of the great questions now agitating the nation."

The businessmen of Boston did not agree so well among themselves or act so decisively. "They would favor any man and any speech which would settle the slavery question and leave commerce unthreatened and unimpaired," one newspaper said, as trading remained slow on the local securities and cotton markets. Millowners, waiting impatiently for a tariff increase, now that the Whigs were in power, could expect none until Congress somehow had disposed of the vexing territorial issues.

"What say our friends in Boston?" Webster asked his scholarly and aristocratic Massachusetts colleague, Representative Robert C. Winthrop, on the latter's return to Washington after a visit home. "I thought them satisfied with the President's policy," Winthrop replied, "and not disposed to press matters to a dangerous pass upon the Wilmot Proviso." This was not very helpful advice, for (to judge from what Southerners were saying) the President's policy itself, if upheld by Congress, would press matters to a dangerous pass.

One group of moneyed men, the holders of debt certificates issued by the former Republic of Texas, felt a special interest in the passage of at least part of the Clay compromise. If the Federal government should take over the Texan debt, their speculation would turn out well. Many of the speculators were, in the words of the banker Jay Cooke, "influential northern men."

Northern property owners as a whole had a tremendous stake in the preservation of peace and union, if some of the Southerners were to be believed. Against the "centrifugal tendencies of locofocoism," of radical Democracy, Northern conservatives must ally themselves with the planters of the South, or so a Florida congressman declared (March 5, 1850). The Union, he told his fellow Whigs from the North, was indispensable to them. "To you it may be necessary to save you from the effects of Socialism, Agrarianism, Fanny Wrightism, Radicalism, Dorrism, and Abolitionism. The *conservatism of slavery* may be necessary to save you from the thousand destructive *isms* infecting the social organization of your section." A dozen years earlier John C. Calhoun had said essentially the same thing.

The Whig party, the party of big businessmen and big slaveholders, long had been the vehicle of conservatism. But the national conservatism of Webster and the North had never harmonized completely with the local conservatism of most of the planters in the South. The growth of antislavery feeling among Northern Whigs made the existing political alliance less and less attractive to Southern party members. Now, with Taylor pointing one way and Clay another, the Whig party seemed near the point of dissolution, and with the loss of this planter-capitalist axis would go a mainstay of the conservative cause, to say nothing of Webster's presidential hopes.

There was no "serious danger," Webster kept telling himself and others as the winter weeks went by. "If, on our side, we keep cool, things will come to no dangerous pass," he said as late as February 16.

Before long he changed his mind, and for good reasons. One by one the Southern states appointed delegates to an all-Southern convention to meet at Nashville in the summer and presumably make plans for a concerted secession movement. The Mississippi legislature, when naming its delegate (March 6), also appropriated two hundred thousand dollars to be used, "in the event of the passage of the Wilmot Proviso," for "necessary measures for protecting the state," that is, for war.

Meanwhile the Southerners in Congress, Whigs and Democrats combining in a sectional bloc, filibustered against the admission of California and demonstrated their power to obstruct not only the President's plan but all legislation of whatever kind. Webster knew most of the Southern senators well, and they showed him the letters they were receiving from their constituents, letters which supported the "most ultra" opinions of the politicians. He came to believe that secession and civil war were real and imminent possibilities.

"I am nearly broken down with labor and anxiety," he confessed to his son (February 24). "I know not how to meet the present emergency, or with what weapons to beat down the Northern and Southern follies, now raging in equal extremes."

2

One thing Webster could do was to make a speech, and he determined to do so, "to make an honest truth-telling speech and a Union speech." While preparing it he conferred privately with various Southern senators, including Calhoun, but no one knew precisely what he was going to say. His Massachusetts colleague Winthrop assumed that he would agree essentially with the administration, and the Washington correspondent of the Boston *Advertiser* predicted (March 4) that he would "take a large view of the state of things" and endorse the principle of the Taylor plan. Like many other Whigs, Webster was trying in fact to ignore the differences between Taylor and Clay, no doubt intending thereby to obscure the party rift.

On March 4 Calhoun, dying of tuberculosis, started to read a speech, then had to sit while it was read for him. He indicated that the Clay compromise was insufficient to secure the interests of the South. The North, he charged, had outstripped the South in population and power because of unfair actions of the Federal government, because of tariffs, land laws, and expenditures on internal improvements. Political parties in the North, catering to the fanaticism of abolitionists, were fast becoming abolitionized, and the Northern people were being convinced that slavery was a sin. In these circumstances disunionism could not be overcome by cries of "the Union, the glorious Union" (Webster's stock in trade) any more than illness could be cured by cries of "health, glorious health." The South must have constitutional guarantees. In a work to be published posthumously, Calhoun was proposing a constitutional amendment giving the United States a dual presidency, one president to be elected by the North and another by the South, each with an independent veto. So far as he was concerned, the alternative for the South was secession, to him a perfectly constitutional and peaceable remedy.

On March 7 Webster rose on the Senate floor, his face unusually stern as he stood for a moment and passed a hand across his forehead. "I wish to speak today, not as a Massachusetts man, nor as a Northern man, but as an American," he said in a conversational tone, low but clear. "I speak today for the preservation of the Union." Then he launched upon his last great performance on the senatorial stage, his gestures becoming increasingly vigorous, his voice swelling till at times the chandeliers seemed to vibrate with his words.

He pled for tolerance. As between the two sections, slavery indeed had become an ethical and even a religious issue, he said. He, for one, believed that slavery was an evil, and Southerners themselves had thought so once. Their opinions had been influenced by their interests: "it was the COTTON interest that gave a new desire to promote slavery." Anyhow, the problem of ethics was too complex to be solved by those who "deal with morals as with mathematics" and "think that what is right may be distinguished from what is wrong with the precision of an algebraic equation." Man's moral duties were numerous and conflicting; "too eager a pursuit" of one of them might lead to violation of others, to disregard of St. Paul's admonition not to "do evil that good may come." There were many evils in the world besides slavery, and one of the worst of them was war.

Having thus dismissed ethical absolutism, Webster proceeded to review and to appraise the specific grievances of both the South and the North.

Southerners like Calhoun charged that "certain operations of the government" had accounted for "the more rapid growth of the North than the South." There was perhaps some truth in this, Webster conceded, but he said it was even more certain that the government had "promoted the increase of the slave interest and the slave territory of the South," as in the acquisition of Florida, Louisiana, and especially Texas.

"Now, as to California and New Mexico," he went on, "I hold slavery to be excluded from those territories by a law even superior to that which admits and sanctions it in Texas." This was the law of nature, of physical geography, he said. Though peonage existed in the lands recently acquired from Mexico, African slavery of the kind familiar in the Southern states could never be successfully implanted there. Therefore, Webster declared, he would not vote for any prohibition (such as the Wilmot Proviso) in a bill for organizing a New Mexican territorial government. "I would not take pains uselessly to reaffirm an ordinance of nature, nor to re-enact the will of God." To do so would only be to "wound the pride" of the Southern people.

Another complaint of the South was the agitation of antislavery societies in the North. These societies, Webster said, had done more harm than good even for the slaves themselves. In the Southern reaction against abolitionism "the bonds of the slaves were bound more firmly than before, their rivets were more strongly fastened." Another complaint was "the violence of the Northern press." Against this, however, Southerners could not look to the Federal government for a remedy. "With all its licentiousness and all its evil, the entire and absolute freedom of the press is essential to the preservation of government on the basis of a free constitution."

The South did have one "solid grievance," one with "just foundation," one "within the redress of the government." Northerners had shown "a disinclination to perform fully their constitutional duties in regard to persons bound to service who have escaped into the free states," said Webster. "In that respect the South, in my judgment, is right and the North is wrong."

But Northerners also had grounds for complaint against the South. They complained, with reason, of the fact that

Southerners no longer regarded slavery as an evil but now regarded it as "an institution to be cherished, and preserved, and extended." Southerners even said that their slaves were better off than Northern workers. This was an insult to a whole people, Webster implied. "Why, who are the laboring people of the North? They are the whole North."

Turning to the question of remedies, Webster said that grievances on either side, so far as they arose from law, could be redressed and ought to be. So far as grievances depended on opinion, they could not be removed by legislation. "All that we can do is to endeavor to allay the agitation, and cultivate a better feeling and more fraternal sentiments between the South and the North."

As for secession, it was no remedy at all. "There can be no such thing as a peaceable secession," said Webster, contradicting Calhoun. "I see that it must produce war, and such a war as I will not describe, *in its twofold character*" (a hint of slave uprisings). Physically, the North and the South could not separate, least of all in the valley of the Mississippi, the home of the future strength of America.

Webster had one last remark, one afterthought, and here at the end he came to the heart of the nation's dilemma, to the question of slavery itself and "the mode of its extinguishment or melioration." He confessed he had nothing to recommend. He could only say that if any gentleman from the South should propose a scheme, "to be carried on by this government upon a large scale, for the transportation of free colored people to any colony or any place in the world," he would support it wholeheartedly no matter what the cost.

When he had finished, the crowd in the Senate chamber

roared its applause, while hundreds pushed their way to his desk to shake his hand and give him their fervent thanks. But the ghostlike Calhoun, as soon as he could make himself heard, feebly expressed his vehement dissent, saying: "No, Sir, the Union *can* be broken." Webster admitted that it could be, but insisted: "That is *revolution* — that is revolution!" In a few minutes the two old antagonists, still respectful of one another, weary after a whole generation of debate, ceased their colloquy.

Though Webster in his speech had mentioned neither Taylor's nor Clay's proposals as such, it could be taken only as an endorsement of those of Clay. Not that he expected, by the sheer force of his argument, to convert Calhoun or other dissenters among his Senate colleagues. He did hope to reach the American people, to influence them, and through them the Congress, in favor of compromise.

Some of his Whig colleagues cautioned him that, if it went to the country just as he had delivered it, the speech would react against the party in every state above the Potomac. So, before publication, he revised it so as to make his lists of Southern and Northern grievances somewhat more balanced. He discreetly struck out a passage in which he had said the money collected by the abolitionists, if rightly spent, would have purchased the freedom of every slave in Maryland. To his list of Northern grievances he added an item concerning the arrest and imprisonment of free colored seamen on Yankee ships visiting Southern ports.

Once the speech was ready in pamphlet form, he franked thousands of copies from Washington while his business friends distributed tens of thousands from Boston and New York. "I do not care what a portion of the press may say," he wrote to one of his friends, "if we can only get the speech into the hands of the people."

Among the most important people of New York the speech proved to be an instant success. The price of United States bonds, which had been falling before March 7, rose sharply thereafter on the metropolitan exchange. Lewis Tappan, one of a tiny abolitionist minority among the businessmen, reported with disgust that "merchants," "brokers," "monied men," and "owners of bank, railroad, and manufacturing stocks" continually quoted excerpts from Webster's address. In individual letters and in one letter signed by several hundred they thanked him for his great effort. "Its tranquillizing effect upon public opinion has been wonderful," one writer said. As a more concrete token of their gratitude a group of businessmen presented to their favorite statesman a handsome gold watch and chain.

From New England he received other commendatory mail, along with it a public letter bearing the signatures of several hundred prominent Bostonians: merchants, scholars, professional men, ministers of the gospel. Many Yankees, however, withheld their praise. Even some of the manufacturers, such as Linus Childs, an official of the Lowell mills, were inclined at first to disapprove of Webster and of compromise. But he could use on them an argument as powerful as any in his speech itself. They desired a new tariff, and they could not get one without the votes of Southern Whigs. These Southerners demanded a price for their aid. "They will not give a single vote for the tariff until this slavery business is settled," Webster reported (May 29) to one of his Boston intimates, Peter

Harvey. "A very leading individual among them told Mr. Childs yesterday that, so far as depended on him, the Lowell mills might and should all stop, unless the North quit this violence of abuse — and showed a disposition to be reasonable in the present exciting questions."

The New England abolitionists, unmoved by economic considerations, kept flailing Webster on account of his speech. The editor of the *Liberator,* William Lloyd Garrison, condemned him as "the great apostate," and the "good gray poet" John Greenleaf Whittier anathematized him as a man whose soul had fled and whose honor had died on March 7, 1850. Somehow the reformers managed to see him as one who lately had been with them, then suddenly had turned renegade.

In truth, he never had espoused their views of slavery, though he always had considered it a moral and social evil, both before and after the firsthand knowledge he gained on his Southern trips in 1847 and 1849. He assumed that after a century or so not only slave labor but Negro labor would disappear from the South, which then would become "a most agreeable region." Pending that happy day he remained, like most Northern politicians of his time, a strict legalist and constitutionalist. Slavery within the Southern states was to him a fact, a disagreeable fact, which the Constitution recognized and with which the Federal government had no right to interfere.

On one point he did reverse himself in the Seventh of March address. Earlier, from the Missouri controversy on, he repeatedly had expressed his fear that slavery, if unhindered, would expand westward even to the Pacific. In 1848, when the Democratic presidential candidate, Lewis Cass, assured Northern voters that slavery could not, for geographical reasons, take root in New Mexico and California, Webster undertook to refute him. After the Seventh of March address Senator Stephen A. Douglas, himself the chief engineer of compromise in 1850, asked ironically why the Massachusetts statesman was so late in discovering the ordinance of nature which interdicted slavery in those territories.

Having belatedly discovered the natural ordinance, Webster stuck manfully to it and boldly denied the charges of inconsistency which came from abolitionists as well as Democrats like Douglas. The question of slavery in the territories, he said in the Senate, in vindication of his Seventh of March address, was "a mere abstraction." He was confident that such an abstraction would not deflect his fellow citizens from the pursuit of their real and substantial economic interests. Commerce, navigation, the fisheries, manufactures, all were suffering because of the sectional disturbance and the congressional impasse. "I cannot conceive," said Webster, "that these great interests would be readily surrendered by the businessmen of the country, the laboring community of the Northern states, to abstractions, to naked possibilities, to idle fears that evils may ensue if a particular abstract measure [the Wilmot Proviso] is not passed. Men must live; to live, they must work."

But he continued to receive denunciations from Northern reformers, who lived by works as well as by work, who pursued abstract ideals in disregard of economic interests. "When I see gentlemen from my own part of the country, no doubt from motives of the highest character and for the most conscientious purposes, not concurring in any of these great questions with myself," he confessed in the

Senate, "I am aware that I am taking on myself an uncommon degree of responsibility." Yet, he said, he could not depart from his own convictions. "My object is peace. My object is reconciliation."

His object was achieved, though imperfectly and only temporarily. He did not succeed in silencing all the "agitators, North and South," or all the "local ideas, North and South," but he helped to rally a majority in both sections to a renewed sense of nationality and of the need for sectional give and take. He did much to create a public spirit in which the Compromise of 1850 could finally be passed and the secession movement of that summer headed off.

3

The veto power of the President stood in the way of the compromise bills until, in July, Taylor suddenly died from the combined effects of his bizarre diet, the Washington heat, and a cholera epidemic. At the funeral his warhorse, Old Whitey, nuzzled up to the coffin as if he knew his late master was there, but General Winfield Scott, Taylor's rival for honors in the Mexican War, who led the funeral procession, gave no comparable demonstration of grief, nor did Senators Cass, Benton, Clay, and Webster among the pallbearers. "If General Taylor had lived we should have had civil war," Webster told a friend a few days afterward.

The new President, Millard Fillmore, a New Yorker, represented the conservative wing of Northern Whigdom. Within a few weeks he reorganized the cabinet, putting

Webster at the head of it as Secretary of State. The new cabinet members were "all National in their sentiments and purposes," as one New York businessman wrote appreciatively to Fillmore. "To you," Webster heard from Caleb Cushing, "it must be a proud triumph to step at once over the heads of your enemies and be giving audience to Mr. Lawrence and the rest."

To Webster another proud triumph was the passage, in September, of the last of the compromise bills. In New York the merchants exulted while a hundred guns at the Battery fired a salute, and throughout the country the popular cry seemed to favor the Union and the Constitution as Webster had expounded them. In Washington Whig and Democratic politicians celebrated drunkenly, and one night a crowd serenaded the Secretary of State while friends held him unsteadily on his feet. "Since the 7th of March there has not been an hour in which I have not felt a 'crushing' weight of anxiety and responsibility," he wrote at a more sober moment. "It is over. My part is acted, and I am satisfied."

Actually it was not over. His real troubles were just beginning. Their source was the new Fugitive Slave Law, which proved to be the crux of the compromise. Southerners announced, through resolutions of their state legislatures, that they would accept the rest of the compromise only on condition that Northerners faithfully observe this part of it.

The law was not the one that Webster himself, while in the Senate, had proposed. His bill would have given alleged runaways the protection of trial by jury. When his bill failed, he voted for and defended the bill that passed without such a guarantee. He deplored the "prejudice" among his own constituents against the reclamation of fugitives, a prejudice arising from the "din and roll and rub-a-dub" of abolitionists who spread "misapprehensions" about the "actual evil." Why, he said, there had not been a case "within the knowledge of this generation" in which a man had been "taken back from Massachusetts into slavery."

Unfortunately for him, the evil soon ceased to be hypothetical. On February 18, 1851, a fugitive from Virginia who had taken the symbolic name of Shadrach was arrested by a United States marshal in Boston. The local abolitionist vigilantes contrived Shadrach's escape. But they were unable to free Thomas Sims, a Negro boy who was seized on the night of April 3, 1852. Sims was shipped back to the South and was publicly whipped on April 19, a date already memorable in Massachusetts history.

In Boston, in Syracuse, in Oberlin, and in other places throughout the North, fleeing slaves were snatched from the hands of Federal authorities and spirited away to freedom. Each slave rescue, mighty propaganda of the deed, heightened the sympathy of Northerners for the anti-slavery cause. Meanwhile *Uncle Tom's Cabin,* even mightier propaganda of the word, detailed the sufferings of the fugitive Eliza for a wide-eyed Northern audience. More and more the people of the North came to believe that there was a "higher law" than the Fugitive Slave Law, a higher law than the Constitution itself.

Against this rising sentiment Webster had to contend. He made the execution of the compromise the main business of his two years as Secretary of State and chief adviser to President Fillmore. The Shadrach rescue he viewed as nothing less than treason, a "foul blot on the good name" of Boston. Assuming some of the duties of the Attorney General, he undertook to see that the Shadrach case and other "rescue cases" should be prosecuted by the "best talent & experience of the bar." Encroaching on the ground of the Postmaster General, he also tried to use the Federal patronage against the troublemakers, among them the postmaster at Lowell, who, he told Fillmore, was "represented to be a brawling abolitionist, preaching daily the duty of resistance to the fugitive slave law."

On a speechmaking tour he carried his defense of the law to the people of upstate New York. "There is but one question in the country now," he said in Buffalo. "Can we preserve the Union . . . not by military power, but by the silken cords of mutual, fraternal, patriotic affection?" The Constitution was the pact of Union, and the return of fugitives was enjoined by the Constitution. "I profess to love liberty as much as any man living," he declared, but only "constitutional liberty," not "that other and higher liberty which disregards the restraints of law and the Constitution."

Northern business interests depended on the maintenance of the Constitution and the preservation of the Union, Webster said in Albany. But what had the abolitionists said in Syracuse and in Boston? "It was this: 'You set up profit against conscience; you set up the means of living: we go for conscience.' " Webster snorted: "That is a flight of fanaticism." The compromise, if right and fair, was "none the worse for being profitable," and the Constitution none the worse for "having been found useful."

The more Webster preached his legalistic doctrine, the more he was excoriated as the chief of all the slave-catchers in the country. So, as the months went by, he played down the theme of law and order and played up his old tune of transcendent Americanism, of cultural expansionism.

"Our system of government is not to be destroyed by *localisms,* North or South," he told the celebrants at a Pilgrim Festival in New York. "No; we have our private opinions, state prejudices, local ideas; but over all, submerging all, *drowning* all, is that great sentiment, that always, and nevertheless, *we are all Americans.*" We must make Americanism prevail throughout America. "It is our duty to carry English principles" — he paused, turning to the minister from England, Sir Henry Bulwer, among his hearers — "I mean, Sir, Anglo-Saxon *American* principles, over the whole continent."

Webster applied that sentiment to Europe as well as America. In the State Department he had inherited a quarrel with the Austrian chargé, the Baron Hülsemann, who objected to the sending of an American emissary to Hungarians in revolt against the Hapsburg regime. To reply to Hülsemann's protests, Webster had his department counselor William Hunter prepare a note "looking," as Hunter said, "both to the foreign affairs and the domestic politics of the United States."

This note acknowledged that the revolutions of 1848 in Hungary and in other countries of Europe had originated, at least in part, in "those great ideas of responsible and popular government" on which the American Constitution itself was founded. The note then gave a gratuitous tweak to the Hapsburg nose. "The power of this republic, at the present moment, is spread over a region one of the richest and most fertile on the globe, and of an extent in comparison with which the possessions of the house of Hapsburg are but as a patch on the earth's surface."

Privately Webster confessed his real motives for the note to Hülsemann. "If you say that my Hülsemann letter is boastful and rough, I shall own the soft impeachment," he wrote to George Ticknor. "My excuse is twofold: 1. I thought it well enough to speak out, and tell the people of Europe who and what we are, and awaken them to a just sense of the unparalleled growth of this country. 2. I wished to write a paper which should touch the national pride, and make a man feel *sheepish* and look *silly* who should speak of disunion."

Webster touched the national pride again when the Hungarian revolutionary leader Louis Kossuth visited the United States as a guest of the American government. At a Washington banquet in Kossuth's honor the Secretary of State himself delivered the main address. The "progress of opinion" was shaking the thrones of tyrants all over the world, he said. "We shall rejoice to see our American model upon the lower Danube and on the mountains of Hungary." A toast: *"Hungarian Independence."*

So, for neither the first nor the last time in American history, support for liberalism abroad was invoked to advance the cause of conservatism at home.

4

One effect of crisis and compromise in 1850, Webster thought, was a "softening of political animosities." He meant a softening of animosities between conservative Democrats and conservative Whigs. "Those who have acted together in this great crisis," he believed, "can never again feel sharp asperities towards one another." As for himself, he could no longer feel in his heart any hostility even toward Senator Cass.

He knew, of course, that there was no such softening of animosities within parties, either Democratic or Whig. After the compromise the Whig party in Massachusetts fell in two, and antislavery Whigs combined with free-soil Democrats to defeat the regular Whig candidates for governor and senator, sending the doctrinaire Charles Sumner to the Senate seat which Webster had vacated.

If many Whigs in the North should behave like that, a "remodelling of parties" was bound to come, Webster predicted. "There must be a Union Party, & an opposing party under some name, I know not what, very likely the Party of Liberty."

A number of Northern businessmen and Southern planters, agreeing with Webster, undertook to organize a bipartisan Union movement. In Pennsylvania, New York, and several Southern states they made considerable headway during the elections of 1851. Thus encouraged, they hoped to present a national Union ticket, headed by Webster, in the presidential election the following year. The New York merchants decided, however, to capture the

regular party if they could, and in March 1852, at the
expense of several thousand dollars, they staged a meeting
to endorse Webster and call for Webster delegates to
the Whig national convention soon to meet in Baltimore.

In Baltimore the first ballot yielded only 29 votes for
Webster, none of them from Southern delegates, to 133
for Fillmore and 131 for Winfield Scott. Since but 147
were necessary for a choice, the Webster men and the Fillmore men could have named a candidate satisfactory to
both if they had combined their votes. They dared not
run the risk, however, of their own delegates breaking
loose in the shuffle and going for Scott. Finally, on the
fifty-third ballot, several men from the Fillmore and Webster ranks did desert to Scott, giving him the nomination.

Though the Whig platform upheld the Compromise of
1850, including the Fugitive Slave Law, the Whig candidate was unsatisfactory to conservative Whigs both North
and South. They had the alternative of deserting to the
Democratic candidate, Franklin Pierce, whom antislavery
people denounced as a doughface, a Northern man with
Southern principles.

Many of the disaffected Whigs determined to go for
Pierce instead of Scott, but others resumed their earlier
schemes for a third party and a third candidate. A rump
convention of the Independent Whigs of Georgia nominated Webster, and so did a national convention of the
American party, with delegates from ten states. Some of
the New York merchants, after failing to carry out their
plans for a national Union convention, attempted to ar-
range a separate Webster electoral ticket for the state of
New York.

Other leaders of the metropolitan business community

hesitated to abandon the Whig party, and they became alarmed at these divisive efforts to nominate Webster, efforts which he neither accepted nor rejected. Several weeks before Election Day a group of his New York friends appealed to him to take a stand. "A public disclaimer from you of any favor towards movements further connecting your name with the coming presidential campaign," these friends urged, is "required by your past and present eminent position whether as a Whig or a Statesman."

In his reply Webster could not conceal his bitterness at the final frustration of his career. "There is no equal number of gentlemen in the United States who possess more of my deep attachment and regard than the signers of your letter," he wrote. "But if I were to do what you suggest, it would gratify not only you and your friends but that great body of implacable enemies who have prevented me from being elected President of the United States."

Privately Webster foretold the election of Pierce and the dissolution of the Whig party. The party, he explained, had begun its "downward course" when it abandoned principle for expediency, when in imitation of its opponents it had turned to "available" men instead of able men, to military heroes like Harrison, Taylor, and now Scott. The new, misguided party leaders had dismissed Webster's advice as that of a man who had "no sympathies with the people" and knew nothing about their wants and tastes. "Now," protested Webster, "I say, with all deference to these young men of the party, that I do know a great deal more about the temper of the American people than they give me credit for, and a great deal more than they know. This one thing I know: that the

American people will not elect General Scott President."
As for himself, if he had a vote to give, he would cast it for
his friendly New Hampshire neighbor, Franklin Pierce.

To the last, Webster clung to the belief that in a democracy like the United States, where property was widely distributed, a conservative party could win a presidential
election with a frankly conservative candidate and platform. He thought the people, having interests to conserve,
could be shown the wisdom of conservatism. True, he had
dabbled in demagoguery while campaigning for a military
hero in 1840, but his heart had not been in it. He had
merely gone along with those other Whig leaders who
seemed to think the party must choose between principles
and majorities. In the end the Whigs possessed neither.

5

Webster was dying. His time had come. He had survived
his three score years and ten, and his physical ailments
were worsening, his hay fever, lumbago, liver complaint,
and chronic diarrhea. No doubt his political disappointment hastened the end. He was himself aware of psycho-
somatic realities, as he indicated not long before his final
illness, while reading a book by a contemporary English
physician, a Dr. Holland. "He has some excellent chapters
upon the effect of the mental affections upon the corporal
system, its diseases, &c.," Webster wrote to his son. "But I
knew all this before Dr. Holland did."

For twenty years it had been his habit, when frustrated
with politics, to look for respite in the avocation of farm-

ing. He owned and operated farms in Illinois, New Hampshire, and Massachusetts. His favorite, his chosen home, was Marshfield, on the coast between Boston and Plymouth. "Oh, Marshfield, Marshfield!" he would cry in Washington when weary of public affairs, or he would say: "The giants grew strong again by touching the earth; the same effect is produced on me by touching the salt seashore." As a boy, he had been happy while evading the chores of the family farm; as a man, he seemingly longed to recover some of the serenity of his boyhood, and tried to do so by devoting his odd hours and days to the agricultural pursuits which, in memory, he associated with that arcadian time.

He took his farming seriously but joyfully. He acquired an intimate knowledge of trees and shrubs, of fruits and vegetables and grains. Fond of oxen and cattle and even pigs, he watched carefully their health and growth and kept close account of expenses and returns. Wherever he traveled he observed with interest the local ways of husbandry, the ditching and tilling in England as well as the "agricultural beauty and richness of the country," the cotton fields and rice plantations and turpentine and cypress swamps of the Southern states. To his farm managers he sent minute directions for the trial of new implements, the use of new fertilizers such as guano and kelp, the proper order in the rotation of crops.

He meant to make his farming pay, and he liked to talk of "a little farm well tilled," but his fancy tastes got the better of him. He imported exotic stock, even llamas from the Andes, and he added to his acres in the hope of establishing a great estate, one comparable to that of his most loved hero, George Washington. His interests as a large-scale experimental farmer help to explain his almost infinite capacity for going through money. But moneymaking was only an incidental object of the master of Marshfield.

Here with his retinue of servants (some of them former slaves he had bought and freed), with his "ladylike wife," with his wealthy cronies from Boston or New York, he vacationed in a style that gave him more real satisfaction than any of his triumphs in the State Department, the Senate, or the Supreme Court. He was, according to one of his visitors, Philip Hone, "the very perfection of a host. At one moment instructive and eloquent, he delights his guests with the charms of his conversation; then, full of life and glee as a boy escaped from school, he sings snatches of songs, tells entertaining stories, and makes bad puns, in which his guests are not behind him." Hone noted (in 1845) that the great, rambling house had been enlarged and beautified, at Webster's direction, and that the library, "in a splendid new wing," was quite as impressive as one would expect.

Here, among his intimates, Webster displayed his whimsical erudition and his intellectual curiosity, discussing the derivation of words like the "rut" of the sea, the origin and naming of the turkey, the question whether shoes were right and left in Shakespeare's time. He expressed also his conventional views of personal morality, views which caused him to be shocked by the reputed wickedness of Lord Byron and by the "abominable transactions" of the Mormons, a "diabolical society of men and women." He expounded his equally conventional religious opinions, deploring the new trend among clergymen who preached to the crowd and not to the individual, who took their texts from the newspapers and not from St. Paul.

Here, at Marshfield, he was a sportsman, rising early to shoot birds in the swamps and to catch fish in the creeks and from the good sloop *Comet* in the bay. On such occasions he dressed "in a loose coat and trousers, with a most picturesque slouched hat, which a Mexican bandit might have coveted." This, the sportsman and gentleman farmer, may have been the true Daniel Webster, or it may have been the actor in another of his roles and careful, as usual, to don a costume appropriate to the part.

Here, home to die in the fall of 1852, he retained his sense of the theatrical to the end. The night he died, October 23, he called the entire household to his bedside and made a speech on the immortality of the soul. Then he dozed off. When he opened his eyes he looked eagerly around and asked: "Have I — wife, son, doctor, friends, are you all here? — have I, on this occasion, said anything unworthy of Daniel Webster?"

I X
Posterity, Its Judgment
1852-1952

"We must take our chance, Sir, as to the light in which posterity will regard us. I do not decline its judgment, nor withhold myself from its scrutiny."

WHILE HE LIVED Daniel Webster enjoyed an Olympian reputation as orator, statesman, and lawyer. Immediately after his death his old acquaintance and opponent William Plumer wrote: "He was in some respects the greatest man which this country ever produced — not in all respects, for he was deficient in that moral energy and indomitable will which carried forward so wonderfully such a man as Jackson, for instance, who was in many other respects so much his inferior." His eulogists, prominent among them Rufus Choate and Edward Everett, who rivaled him in oratorical fame, conceded no such defect as they commemorated him in 1852 and again and again in after years.

In the midst of the general mourning ("the sensation produced through the whole country by his death," said Plumer, "is the strongest I have ever witnessed in the case of any public man") the Reverend Theodore Parker

preached at the Melodeon, in Boston, a most remarkable
obituary sermon. Sounding like the Almighty in final
judgment on a sinner, Parker declaimed for three hours
upon what was afterward printed as *A Discourse Occa-
sioned by the Death of Daniel Webster*. In it he granted
Webster certain elements of greatness but, taking the
Seventh of March address as a revelation of the essential
man, contended that his career had come to ruin because
of his character defects. Selfish, egotistical, excessively ambitious, Webster had done more than any man alive to
"debauch the conscience of the nation."

This theme the pioneer of American popular biographers, James Parton, elaborated in a magazine sketch published in 1865. Webster, according to Parton, had been en-
dowed with almost every quality of greatness except moral
strength. He lusted after the presidency, listened eagerly
to his many flatterers, blackmailed the capitalists of Boston and New York, and lost his independence because of
his loose financial habits. After reaching the glorious
height of his career with the Reply to Hayne, he decayed
within while outwardly shining in the afterglow of former
brilliance until, all at once, the inner rottenness was ex-
posed on that fateful Seventh of March.

John Quincy Adams spoke from the grave to reinforce
that estimate when his memoirs were published in the
1870's. Adams once had written of "the gigantic intellect,
the envious temper, the ravenous ambition, and the rotten
heart of Daniel Webster." Henry Cabot Lodge, himself
destined to become a famous senator from Massachusetts,
took his cue from Parton and from abolitionists still living, such as James Russell Lowell and William Lloyd Garrison, when, around the centenary of Webster's birth, he

prepared the most widely read biography of the man.

While the Seventh of March was most remembered, the Reply to Hayne was never quite forgotten, and during the second generation after Webster's death his fame as a nationalist came to prevail over his disrepute as a compromiser. Even Parton and Lodge conceeded that, for all his moral failure, he had served his country well by fixing the principles of Union so firmly in the American mind as to sustain the people through four years of civil war. Afterward one Union veteran recalled that while on sentinel duty, he had kept up his courage by reciting Webster's words, "Liberty and Union, now and forever, one and inseparable," and another said: "Webster shotted our guns." George F. Hoar, Lodge's colleague as senator from Massachusetts, declared that Webster's place in history was that of "a public teacher, guiding the thought and inspiring the emotions of his countrymen when the issues on which hung the fate of the Republic were being determined."

During the war President Lincoln once expressed a rather harsh opinion of Webster. In a cabinet conversation the President agreed with his Secretary of State, William H. Seward, that both Webster and Clay had been hard and selfish leaders whose individual ambitions contributed to the ruin of the Whig party. Yet, on the issues of slavery and Union, Lincoln repeatedly spoke in Websterian echoes and acted in a Websterian spirit. The memorable phrase at Gettysburg — "of the people, by the people, for the people" — was a terse expression of what Webster had said in *McCulloch* v. *Maryland* and in the Reply to Hayne. The "last hopes of mankind," Webster said in 1825, rested on the success of the Union, the American experiment in popular government. Unless the experiment succeeded and the Union was saved, Lincoln said in 1862, we would lose the "last best hope of earth." Physically speaking, "we cannot separate," Webster insisted in 1850; Lincoln did the same in 1861. To Webster the question of slavery in the territories was a "mere abstraction," and to Lincoln the question whether the seceded states were in or out of the Union, after Appomattox, was a "merely pernicious abstraction." Webster confessed he had no plan for disposing of slavery, but he expected it to disappear in a century or so, and he was willing to support a program for colonizing freed Negroes outside the country. Lincoln did propose an emancipation plan, but he expected the process to take many years at best, and he, too, favored settling freedmen in foreign lands.

After Lincoln's assassination and the Radicals' rise to power, the leaders of the Republican party had no use for the memory of Webster. Still later, after the end of Radical Reconstruction, they began to make room for him in the party pantheon. That Republican of Republicans, James G. Blaine, when composing his *Twenty Years of Congress* in the 1880's, gave Webster a posthumous award of honorary membership in the party. Blaine recalled that in 1861 the Republicans in the Senate, even Charles Sumner, implicitly had endorsed Webster's law-of-nature thesis when they admitted Colorado and Nevada as territories without any prohibition of slavery. Yet these same men, "who agreed in 1861 to abandon the Wilmot Proviso," had, "in 1850, heaped reproach upon Mr. Webster for not insisting upon the same principle for the same territory."

Among Blaine's contemporaries, few scholars adopted

his view of the rightness of Webster's stand on the issue
of slavery in the territories. But a time came when most
historians agreed with Webster (and with Blaine). The
mid-twentieth-century "revisionists" of Civil War history
maintained that the war, the work of a "blundering
generation," came as the result of excitement North and
South over an unreal issue, unreal because no matter what
Congress or the Supreme Court might decide, the territories were geographically unsuited for the Southern slave
economy. Whether correct or not, revisionism was essentially a Websterian interpretation of the Civil War,
though Webster has not been given credit for inspiring it.

Meanwhile, by the turn of the century, Webster had
attained a near apotheosis in the popular imagination. To
schoolboys brought up on works of oratory, his name like
that of his distant cousin Noah became familiar from the
standard textbooks. In the minds of most Americans he
was the foremost of the great triumvirate of bygone statesmen: Webster, Calhoun, and Clay. The distinguished
Englishman James Bryce, in *The American Commonwealth,* first published in 1888 and widely used thereafter
as a textbook, devoted a chapter to explaining "Why
Great Men Are Seldom Chosen Presidents," and he cited
the famous trio as examples of great men whom the electorate had bypassed for mediocrities. In 1900, when a presumably knowledgeable group of electors first balloted on
candidates for New York University's new Hall of Fame,
Washington ranked at the top with ninety-seven votes
and Webster tied Lincoln for second place with ninety-
six.

After another fifty years Webster's memory was threatened with what was worse than the early obloquy, obliv-

ion. True, historians and biographers wrote as much about him after 1900 as before, but schoolchildren learned less and less, until at last a generation of Americans grew up that knew him not. Many of them did know a fictional character bearing his name, for they had read Stephen Vincent Benét's story of "The Devil and Daniel Webster," or they had seen the movie. In Benét's delightful yarn Webster out-argues the Devil before a jury of long-dead Revolutionary figures and breaks a contract which a New Hampshire farmer unwisely had made. Here Benét carried literary license too far. As Arthur M. Schlesinger, Jr., pointed out, a Yankee farmer conceivably might have entered into a pact with the Devil, and a dozen Revolutionary shades might have been assembled as jurymen, but in real life Daniel Webster would never have been found arguing against the sanctity of contract.

2

That men's opinions are influenced by their interests, Webster himself declared. As an instance, he pointed to the South, where, he said, the cotton interest had turned the people from an antislavery to a proslavery consensus. He never confessed that, likewise, the manufacturing interest had turned his own thinking from free trade to protectionism, or that the commercial interest had led him to his conclusion of 1850: that Congress need not legislate slavery out of the territories since God already had done so. Yet, from first to last, his speeches played continually upon variations of a single dominant theme —

the nexus between government and the economy, between politics and interests.

As the economic empire of his clients and constituents widened, so did his concept of nationality and Federal power. When, at the beginning of his Washington career, he spoke pre-eminently for a single parochial group, the shipowners of New Hampshire, he resisted national action which they considered harmful to their affairs, and he went to extremes in defending state rights. After the War of 1812, as the spokesman for corporations engaging in interstate business, he no longer defended but sought to delimit the powers of the states.

When, with the expansion of the Northern business community, a currency and credit system adequate for payments over a wide area was needed, he espoused wholeheartedly the cause, to which at first he had given only qualified support, of a national bank. He was dubious about the constitutionality of protective tariffs when New Englanders first began to invest heavily in textile mills; then, when they had invested enough to make their interest the region's dominant one, he found ample authority in the constitutional clauses on taxation and, better yet, the regulation of commerce.

As manufacturers came to produce much more than a local market could consume, he saw both economic and constitutional justification for Federal expenditures to widen the market by means of highways, river and harbor improvements, and canals. Once there had arisen an Anglo-American community of economic interest, based on a mutually profitable exchange of capital and manufactured goods for raw materials, he championed an appropriate program of conciliatory diplomacy and co-

operative imperialism. And, at last, when the merchants of
New York feared secession and the loss of Southern trade,
he responded to what they conceived to be their immediate interest as he pled for sectional compromise to save
the Union.

Except perhaps at the very beginning, Webster did
not simply mirror the outlook of one particular group.
Rather, his reflection of economic interests often was
blurred because of conflicting loyalties and personal ambition.

With the growth of manufactures and the disruption of
the Federalist party, he faced the task of reconciling or
evading the contradictory demands of overseas commerce
and domestic industry. After manufacturing and protectionism had come to predominate in New England, his
problem was simplified for a time, and during the nullification crisis not only New England but the whole North
was practically as one in acclaiming him.

Then complications reappeared. In the war between
the Jackson administration and the Bank of the United
States he had to choose between the wishes of his employer Biddle and his own presidential prospects as they
might be furthered by a rapprochement with Jackson.
And when his rivals for Jackson's favor ended this dilemma for him, he still had to choose between the interests of Boston businessmen, who urged moderation upon
Biddle, and those of the banker himself, who continued
to press his financial warfare against the administration.

Again, the presidential hopes of Webster and his rivalry
with Clay kept him in Tyler's cabinet while the interests
of Boston business, as interpreted by Abbott Lawrence
and other Clayites, required that he resign. Even his busi-

nessman's treaty with Lord Ashburton did not suffice to justify him in the eyes of such men as Lawrence.

Worst of all for Webster, the Whig party of Massachusetts and to some extent the Boston business community itself began after the Mexican War to divide into "cotton" and "conscience" factions. Many of the New York merchants seemed momentarily to favor conscience and free soil. By 1850, however, most of the business leaders of Boston and almost all of those of New York had swung to cotton and to compromise. At the moment the desires of his wealthy friends and the dictates of his own ambition coincided in impelling Webster to take the stand he did. But his loyalty to big business and his presidential aims became incompatible when Northerners reacted violently against the Fugitive Slave Law.

At the end he devoted himself to what most of the Northern capitalists considered their basic interest — an understanding with Southern planters to preserve law and order along with the Union and to make private property secure — as against what seemed to him the unfounded concern of many Northerners for freedom in the territories.

Throughout his career as a nationalist, Webster maintained that the interests of New England and of the nation as a whole were identical, that the manufacturing interest was a general interest. No doubt he sincerely believed so, though he was capable at times of saying things he knew to be untrue, as when he denied that Biddle was to blame for the financial stringency of 1834. There is little reason to suppose, however, that he arrived at his view of the general welfare from a detached appraisal of the country's needs. There is much reason to believe that

he was led to it by his political and pecuniary connection
with the merchants and manufacturers themselves, a
connection which his upbringing, his personality, and his
legal skill made natural if not inevitable. The pecuniary
inspiration of his ideas does not, in itself, discredit them,
though they cannot be appraised intelligently without
some consideration of the circumstances in which they
were put forth.

3

In judging Webster's career, most important to posterity during the first century after his death were his policies regarding slavery and the Union. More relevant to
Americans during the second century, though not much
appreciated by them, was the general pattern of his conservative thought. Derived in part from the ideas of old
Federalists like John Adams, it had changed from time to
time, at least in details, as Webster developed and expounded it over a period of thirty years. Yet, on the
whole, his thinking was remarkable more for its essential
consistency than for its occasional contradictions.

Power follows property: the two must go together if
there is to be a stable, representative government. This,
though unoriginal with Webster, was the first axiom of
his political thinking from 1820 on. Those who run society's affairs, he maintained, must possess a stake in society. At first he stressed the need for limiting the rights
of governance to those with property; later, following the
democratic extension of the suffrage, he emphasized the

necessity of seeing that property was distributed among the widened electorate. His means of diffusing property — by tariffs, Federal expenditures on internal improvements, and a national bank — may or may not have been sincere and realistic. But he did not violate the logic of his axiom.

He also assumed that, under certain conditions, a harmony of interests could be maintained among the different occupational groups in an increasingly complex society. He never abandoned this assumption, though he did change the conditions. At first he argued that the prerequisite of harmony was a policy of *laissez faire,* and he warned that governmental intervention to aid agriculture, commerce, or manufactures would provoke dangerous struggles for political favor, and — more specifically — that tariff benefits for manufacturing would give rise to a propertyless class of factory workers and produce the most dangerous conflict of all. Later, when industrialism had arrived, he insisted that government must intervene. By proper fiscal policies it could and must encourage enterprise, keep opportunities open and wages high, and make possible that distribution of ownership which he considered indispensable to social harmony.

Mechanical invention, Webster came to believe, would almost automatically improve the human lot. In particular, the application of steam to manufacturing and transportation would raise the status of the common man and bring classes, sections, and nations together in mutual understanding and respect. This faith in material progress enabled Webster comfortably and with easy conscience to disregard contemporary demands for social reform. He possessed little empathy; as Francis Lieber said, he had no feeling for the "massive movements" of the people. He was humane but not humanitarian.

To him the going system of American society and government, though destined to function better and better as time and technology did their work, seemed meanwhile incapable of improvement by direct tinkering. The Constitution, *as it was,* appeared to be perfect. Its grants of power were broad enough to authorize the economic program which national prosperity required, and its restraints upon the people were strict enough to forestall democratic excesses and guarantee the rights of property. The people only needed, first, to understand the Constitution as it was and, second, to will and act in accordance with their understanding.

Hence Webster emphasized that the people must have religion, morality, and education, all of a proper sort. Religion to him was in itself a private and not a public matter. It concerned the relationship of an individual with God, not the relationship of man to man or group to group on earth. It should act more as an anodyne than as a stimulant. Likewise morality, though politically relevant, was in itself personal rather than social. And it was negative rather than affirmative. Education should inculcate sound morals, as thus conceived, and it should instill a knowledge of the beauties of the constitutional system.

While advocating a national conservatism for the United States, Webster applauded the cause of national liberalism in Europe. There was no real contradiction in his doing so, for by European standards his conservatism was liberal enough. He was seeking to spread abroad the blessings of his brand of Americanism, both because he sincerely believed in it and because, at times, he found it a useful expedient for counteracting divisive tendencies at home. Though a nationalist, he was never a jingo, even in his bombastic Hülsemann note. He always decried the Manifest Destiny of the Democrats, with its anti-British and militaristic implications. In its place he prophesied an American Destiny even grander, though less bloody, involving a peaceful conquest of the world by Anglo-American ideals.

Expansive but peaceful Americanism, popular self-discipline, Constitution worship, beneficent technology, realizable harmony of group interests, and power tied to property — such were the elements of Webster's political philosophy in its broadest sense. He never bothered to systematize that philosophy: he was engaged not in scholarly speculation but in forensic combat. Nevertheless the general pattern of his thinking, abstracted from dozens of scattered arguments, does make a coherent whole. Often he applied the word *conservative* to his position, and when politics required him to use *democratic* or *democracy,* he defined those words to fit his conservative proclivities. He was pre-eminently the exponent of American political conservatism as it existed during the second quarter of the nineteenth century.

At most points he did not differ from the liberals of his time, if such Whigs as John Quincy Adams or Theodore Parker may be taken as representative of contemporary liberalism in politics. The biggest difference between him and them arose on the questions of reform and civil liberties, especially as these related to slavery. If no slavery issue had existed, Webster and the liberals of this kind need never have parted as they did. He regularly praised the freedoms in the bill of rights and, even on March 7,

1850, refused to consider any curbs on the press, flagitiously irresponsible though he considered it. But he insisted upon observance of constitutional duties as well as rights, and his undeviating devotion to legalities, and of course to the interests served by them, led him to an illiberal stand upon the Fugitive Slave Law.

On the slavery question the Jacksonian left wing was, before but not after the Mexican War, nearer to him than to Adams or Parker, nearer to the conservatives than to the liberals. On other issues, however, these radicals stood very far from Webster. They generally supposed that group interests were basically contradictory rather than harmonious, at least the interests of capital and labor. Exalting the principle of *laissez faire,* they urged the separation of government and business. And they harped upon the primacy of human as opposed to property rights — a distinction which made little sense to Webster.

On the conflict of interests, though not on human rights, John C. Calhoun agreed with Jacksonian radicalism and not with Websterian conservatism. Calhoun spoke of his own political system as "conservative," but its spirit was parochial rather than national and reactionary rather than anything else. Where Webster deplored slavery, Calhoun praised it as a "positive good," and he was far less willing than Webster to welcome technological change. Calhoun feared that mechanical progress would provoke dangerous "convulsions" unless political science advanced to head them off. By political science he meant his own peculiar doctrine of the "concurrent majority," a doctrine designed to give to a particular minority, the planter class, a veto on national legislation. He believed in government by property, as Webster also did. But Web-

ster, by presupposing a diffusion of ownership, could reconcile property government with popular government;
Calhoun could not, supposing as he did that capitalist society was bound to divide into the propertyless many and
the propertied few. Year in and year out Calhoun hoped
for an effective alliance between planters and capitalists
against what he assumed to be their rising foe, the working class. He kept awaiting a revolutionary crisis which
would bring together, on his own terms, the "gentlemen"
of the North and of the South.

Webster, as a national conservative, could not accept
Calhoun's terms, based as they were upon an extreme
conception of the rights of states. Yet, as a leader of the
Whig party, itself a partial planter-capitalist combination
in politics, Webster for many years did adhere to the
general principle of gentlemanly co-operation across the
Mason-Dixon line. And when the sectional showdown
came, in 1850, he was ready to abandon the old Whig
organization and form a new, more frankly conservative
lignment on the Union issue. Radical Democrats were
joining liberal Whigs on the platform of free soil; conservative Whigs, he thought, should join proslavery Democrats on the platform of compromise.

If a party broadly inclusive of capitalists and planters
could have been solidified, there would have been no
Civil War, or if war nevertheless had come, it would have
been more truly a class conflict, less complicated and ob-
scured by geographical lines than it actually was. War and
Reconstruction drove deeper the wedge which the prewar
controversy had started between Northern and Southern
conservatives. They arranged an understanding but not a
party merger in the deal of 1877 by which Southern Dem-

ocrats conceded the election of a Republican President, despite his very dubious electoral majority, and Republicans abandoned their Southern wards and allies, the former slaves. A hoped-for intersectional party of conservatives did not materialize at that time. Several decades later, despite repeated gestures in its direction, such a party had not yet appeared.

4

Webster's national conservatism, a response to the political needs of the business community in the first half of the nineteenth century, contained much to serve the needs of business in the second half of the twentieth century. So, of course, did the philosophy of Alexander Hamilton, a thinker who made fewer concessions to the democratic notion of rule by the people — that "great beast." Webster, contending for popular favor in the age of Jacksonian Democracy, adapted his ideas as well as his phrases to the increasing self-consciousness of the theoretically sovereign public. For that very reason, his formulation of conservative thought was in many ways more useful than Hamilton's to latter-day businessmen.

As a prophet of usable conservatism, however, neither Webster nor Hamilton was, at the middle of the twentieth century, so fervently invoked as one of Webster's contemporaries — Calhoun. Calhoun's doctrine of concurrent majorities had become more timely than ever, according to a growing school of neo-Calhounites. They found in his doctrine the unwritten rules by which American politics was being carried on a century after his death. The essence of his theory, they said, was not nullification itself but the general idea that every major interest group in the country — business, labor, agriculture, even the Church, even racial or ethnic minorities — should have some kind of veto in national politics. And, according to the new interpreters of Calhoun, every one of these groups actually did exercise such a veto, whether through congressional blocs or lobbies, through administrative agencies, or through party conventions at which dissenting factions were heard and heeded in the privacy of the traditional smoke-filled room. Though some of the neo-Calhounites thought of themselves as liberals, most of them were really conservatives, economic or religious.

Whatever their leanings, they were mistaken both about Calhoun's meaning in his time and about the ways of American politics and government in their own. In their time politicians and pressure groups normally did *not* arrive at policies by unanimous agreement, did *not* allow a "veto" to every major interest. Politicians and pressure groups acted on the basis of a working majority, which they achieved through a combination of several, but not necessarily all, big minorities. In Calhoun's day they did essentially the same thing. But Calhoun did not endorse the logrolling process or the "numerical majority" which it produced. Quite the contrary. He insisted on complete unanimity, or at least on an absolute veto for one particular interest, that of the slaveholders. He sought to establish such a veto constitutionally by his schemes for nullification and the dual presidency, and politically by his efforts to create a sectional party, a solid South.

Whenever, in the twentieth century, disaffected Southerners raised the cry of state rights, or filibustered against Federal legislation designed to protect the Negro, or attempted such experiments as that of the Dixiecratic party, they were carrying on in the spirit though not necessarily in the letter of Calhoun's political philosophy. So were conservatives either North or South whenever they drew together against a supposed threat of class revolt or labor radicalism.

More often, however, the business community as a whole pursued the way of Webster, not that of Calhoun. Like Webster, the business spokesmen of a later century favored various forms of government aid to corporate enterprise, though they pretended to believe in the separation of government and business, while he renounced the whole doctrine of *laissez faire*. Like him, they generally denied the existence, in America, of discernible class lines or even of social classes, to say nothing of class conflicts, except perhaps as class-consciousness might be artificially aroused by a demogogic President — by a Franklin Roose· velt or a Truman as, in Webster's view, by a Jackson or a Polk. Like Webster, later businessmen and business politicians assumed that their interest was a general interest, that what helped business helped everybody. Like him, they identified their program with the American way and condemned that of their opponents as un-American. Like him, many though by no means all resisted war and the postwar expedient of winning presidential elections with military heroes. The Robert A. Taft of 1952, though he had less eloquence and more integrity, occupied a position much like that of the Daniel Webster of 1852.

After more than a century many of Webster's speeches on public issues, with only a word changed here and there, would have served conservative politicians admirably in speaking on the issues of their time. But these politicians seldom quoted Webster or even mentioned him. He was the forgotten man of American conservatism.

A Note on the Sources

THERE ARE very few Americans about whom more
has been written than about Daniel Webster, but almost no
attention has been paid to his conservative philosophy as a
whole, though his legal and constitutional views have been
repeatedly analyzed and a monograph has been produced on
Daniel Webster as an Economist, by Robert L. Carey (1929).
In the second volume of *Main Currents in American Thought*
(1927) Vernon L. Parrington gives a fragmentary account of
Webster's conservatism, and in *The Age of Jackson* (1945) Arthur M. Schlesinger, Jr., touches upon the subject incidentally.
Though both Parrington and Schlesinger provide valuable in-
sights, neither of them considers Webster's thinking after 1820
as worth serious analysis, and Schlesinger misconstrues Calhoun
and Calhounism.

To find what Webster actually thought and said, one must
go to his *Works,* which make surprisingly good reading. The
eighteen volumes of the National Edition (1903) are fairly complete. They may be supplemented by the *Letters of Daniel
Webster,* edited by C. H. Van Tyne (1902).

The standard life is that by Claude M. Fuess (2 vols., 1930);
it contains an extensive bibliography. Still useful at certain
points is the authorized biography by George T. Curtis (2 vols.,
1872). Also valuable, if used with caution, are the anecdotal
reminiscences of Webster by his acquaintances: Charles W.
March (1850 and 1852), Charles Lanman (1852), and Peter
Harvey (1877).

Other writings by contemporaries of Webster which throw varying degrees of light upon his career include the following: *Memoirs of John Quincy Adams,* edited by Charles Francis Adams (12 vols., 1874-1877); the memoirs of Thomas Hart Benton, entitled *Thirty Years' View* (2 vols., 1854-1856); *Correspondence of Nicholas Biddle,* edited by Reginald C. McGrane (1919); *Diary of Philip Hone,* edited by Bayard Tuckerman (2 vols., 1889), also available in a more recent edition by Allan Nevins; *Diary and Correspondence of the Late Amos Lawrence,* edited by William R. Lawrence (1855); and *Life and Letters of Harrison Gray Otis,* edited by Samuel E. Morison (2 vols., 1913).

Among the relevant biographies of Webster's contemporaries may be mentioned Robert C. Winthrop's sketch of Nathan Appleton in the Massachusetts Historical Society *Proceedings* for 1860-1862; Charles M. Wiltse's *John C. Calhoun* (3 vols., 1944-1951); George R. Poage's *Henry Clay and the Whig Party* (1936); Hamilton A. Hill's *Memoir of Abbott Lawrence* (1883); Albert J. Beveridge's *Life of John Marshall* (4 vols., 1916-1919); Robert C. Winthrop, Jr.'s *Memoir of Robert C. Winthrop* (1897); and John A. Garraty's *Silas Wright* (1949).

Of the numerous contemporary travelers' accounts, two are especially rewarding to the reader interested in Webster and his rivals. One is the well-known and justly celebrated *Retrospect of Western Travel* by Harriet Martineau (2 vols., 1838). The other is the perceptive but rather neglected report on *Men and Manners in America* by Thomas Hamilton (1834).

There is not room here to mention all the monographs that deal with particular phases of Webster's career or that illuminate the political and economic backgrounds of it, but a dozen of the books and articles most useful for the present study may be listed: Eber M. Carroll, *Origins of the Whig Party* (1925); Richard N. Current, "John C. Calhoun, Philosopher of Reaction," *Antioch Review,* Summer, 1943, and "Webster's Propaganda and the Ashburton Treaty," *Mississippi Valley Historical Review,* September, 1947; Arthur B. Darling, *Political Changes in Massachusetts, 1824-1848* (1925); Philip S. Foner, *Business & Slavery* (1941); Herbert D. Foster, "Webster's Seventh of March Speech and the Secession Movement, 1850," *American Historical Review,* January, 1922; Oscar and Mary Handlin, *Commonwealth* (1947); Samuel E. Morison, *Maritime History of Massachusetts* (1921); John M. Shirley, *The Dartmouth College Causes* (1879); Edward Stanwood, *American Tariff Controversies* (2 vols., 1903); Frederick J. Turner, *The United States, 1830-1850* (1935); Caroline F. Ware, *The Early New England Cotton Manufacture* (1931).

Index